THE DISSOLUTION OF TRUTH

TERRY E. LURSEN

TEL PUBLISHING

HUNTERSVILLE, NC

TEL Publishing

Huntersville, NC

www.perspectivesintruth.com

The Dissolution of Truth

Copyright © 2016 by Terry E. Lursen
Cover Design: Stephen Lursen Art
Published by: TEL Publishing

ISBN: 978-09910989-8-9

All rights reserved. No part of this publication may be reproduced or transmitted in any form without the prior written permission of the copyright owner.

Scripture taken from the New King James Version ™. Copyright © 1982 by Thomas Nelson, Inc. Used by permission. All rights reserved.

Library of Congress Cataloging-in-Publication Data

Lursen, Terry E., 1957 –

The dissolution of truth

Library of Congress Control Number: 2016908179

Contents

Preface	7
The Dissolution of Truth	9
Reflexivity Exposed	12
Truth	17
The Subversion of Truth	23
The Power of Charismatic Personalities	28
Kings and Pawns	32
The Value of Truth	41
The Importunity of a Lie	44
The Power of Perspective	47
Change	50
Social Liberalism	51
Defying Ubiquity	56
Speaking the Truth on Marriage	60
Led By Convictions	63
Who Instituted Marriage?	67
The Unbecoming of America	69
On Personal Relationships	74
The Dynamics of Spiritual Truth	79
Apparent Contradictions	84
Believing Unbelief	87
On Being Nefarious	89
Peace – The Treasure That You Seek	92
Heighten the Sight	96

The Great Illusion	99
The Opportunity of a Seed	104
Amendment I of the Constitution of the United States of America	110
Obama's Evisceration of God from the Populace	114
Church and State	116
The Egregious Moment	120
The Immoral Leader	121
Homosexuality and Christianity	123
The Philosophy of the Gilded Mind	132
Initializing Freedom	136
The Certain Uncertainty of Man	139
Abortion Is Murder	145
The Parable of the Indiscernible Palate	147
The Author of Marriage	149
The Consequence of Corruption	150
A True Leader Must Have Courage	154
A Sphere of Influence	156
References - Footnotes	158
Bibliography	160

The Philosophical Spirit

The philosophical spirit, that to which I implore and am designed to be... the dialectic, always searching for the truth of the matter, knowing that the absolute exists for He Who is my Creator gave me the heart to feel, the mind to think, the mouth to speak, the ears to listen and the spirit to know Him and to wait on Him for what He has to say in all things...let him who thinks he sees, really see and let him who thinks he hears, truly understand.

"The spirit of dogmatism, whether it is intellectualist or pragmatic, is a spirit of systemization which claims to formulate truth, to comprehend it in a coherent whole and defend it; which claims to have found truth rather than to be seeking it; which is less critical of itself than of its opponents. The philosophical spirit, on the other hand, has a sense of wonder, a sense of the limitations of knowledge and the poverty of the human mind. It never gives up on the quest for truth, but determines to go on pursuing truth even though it knows that it will never completely attain to this in any sphere. It knows that there is no greater obstacle than the conviction that one possesses the truth. It has a sense of true criticism, which is not only compatible with faith and with science, but also necessary to both."   --- Dr. Paul Tournier, A Person Reborn

'Tis a thinking man's dream to think a thought that has never been thought. www.perspectivesintruth.com

Preface

In these United States of America, we are all responsible. I, personally, have waited too long to speak, waiting on others to speak for me. Have I been shut up, or, have I withdrawn to my own quarters to stew about what has been, what is and worry about what is going to be? I have made my decisions, and I, alone, am responsible for them. I have no one to blame but myself for what I allow. I have been moved by my circumstances, oftentimes, beyond my control. I have, at times, fought against my circumstances and kicked against the pricks only to bloody myself, or my family.

Oswald Chambers says that we are made up of a series of moral choices. We make decisions every day. These decisions benefit us, or defeat us, and in the ensuing moments following a made decision we usually know what we have done to ourselves. We cannot blame others for what we do to ourselves, nor can we blame others when we refuse to speak up when we see injustice in the land. The fear of becoming a social pariah is evident when we choose to refrain from speaking when we see the indulgence of our leaders. We want to believe that things are not as they seem to be and in our refusal to acknowledge what truly is, we abrogate ourselves to that substitutionary layer of darkness over light.

We shield our eyes in disbelief of what is, not really wanting to know because, after all, what can we do? What can one person do? It has been attributed to Edmund Burke the statement, "The only thing necessary for the triumph of evil is for good men to do nothing."

At this juncture, this is where the adversary is at his best; to call the individual, 'not good', 'not worthy'. . . in the depths of his heart. And, the individual believes the deception and the lie, rather than the Author Who called His Creation, "Good". If I believe there is no good in me, then, I am unworthy, I have nothing to say, and, worse, no one willing to listen to me. Whose report will I believe?

The construct of anger is the promulgation of antipathy. Clearly stated, I will be willing to speak up and make a statement of righteousness when what I see is so repugnant to me that it angers me and will not let me go.

It is here that I find...I am.

The Dissolution of Truth

The dissolution of truth is a social construct resulting from the annihilation of the absolute leading to immoral social decay. The powers over the liberal agenda use the immorality to further their means towards socialistic a priori (knowledge known implicitly within the group).

Within this group there are no absolutes. Their truth is fiction, untenable, and unexplainable. All are distractions from the undercurrent of the soul of America's destruction and yet they personally believe that theirs is a form of patriotism par excellence. The leaders are refractory, compelled by their selfish greed for power and deluded by their beliefs. Their views are supported by their need to control all and replace truth and reality with their versions of perceptions.

Their leaders are unaccountable and uncooperative. They blame others for their actions, or, their lack of action. They are not responsible and lead others to persecute the opposition for holding them accountable and/or merely having opposing beliefs.

"...a persecutor is an abominable character. Wherefore those who allow of perfect immateriality, without comprehending it, should have tolerated those who rejected it, because they did not comprehend it. Those who have refused God the power of animating the unknown being called matter, should have also tolerated those who have not dared to divest God of His power; for it is very scandalous to hate one another for syllogisms." [1]

The leading of others to hate with racial hate leads only to more and more racism leading ultimately to division and the propensity to violence. The leading of others to despise another's beliefs and so despise the person to hatred who believes differently than you is abhorrent. This, too, is a distraction from the power they wield over their populace to manipulate them to move to action from what is actually in their (the leaders) hearts.

Their views are implacable as they enrich themselves at the expense of the entire populace while impoverishing the people that support their beliefs. They live in denial to the perception that everyone that follows them should live as they do, but cannot, because the leaders have become enriched while the followers have become poorer.

They lead a generation of people who live for handouts of power, wealth of varying types, rights to live immorally, housing, food, and, now, health insurance. They give away what is not theirs to give and benefit from the financial and social theft of the future of our children.

They have to abolish truth and reason as truth and reason cannot exist in the place of promiscuity. Thus, the dissolution of truth is the foundation of the social construct of the liberal, progressive agenda and their way of thought. Perhaps it is easier understood to view the liberal agenda thinker as the child who becomes the voracious bully on the school playground taking more and more ground for his own and dares the others to do something about it. And I, like many other right thinkers have acquiesce to their way and modes of operation, like the pouters on the playground who want to run and tell

The Dissolution of Truth

the teacher about the bully. But, the teacher says, 'Take care of it yourself.'

But there is at least one more side to the liberal expectation and that is the idea of pluralism, both in politics and religion. Religious pluralism is the idea that all religions are equal to one another, including Christianity. The "Pluralism Project" at Harvard University touts as much. This project also includes satan worship and atheism in its long list of global religions that are all deemed equal, even though their leaders know that Jesus Christ professed, "I am the way, the truth and the life...no man comes to the Father unless he comes by Me." How can any religion be equal to the One True LORD? Yet, in their intellectual view, all are equal. Diversity is not enough for them, it has to be a sense of forced tolerance and, as such, people must believe what they beleive and we all just need to get along with all.

But I say, stand your ground, no more taking over. Stand your ground in your mind and heart, in your home, in your school and in your business. It is time to make clear the paths of Truth with clear and sustainable definitions of what is and what is not.

Reflexivity Exposed

Inventive thought perpetuated as new ideas, or, revelation, provide the breeding ground for home-grown truth. Men believe that they create their own truth within the confines of their arenas, no matter how small, or large, they may find their arena to be. On the politician's stage, as well as, some pulpits, the conceptualization of thought is found to be a substitutionary layer over the Constitution of the United States and even the Holy Scriptures as an astigmatism what truly is. The conception of a perspective presented as interpretation or revelation is the result of the human spirit joining with a spirit manifesting as thought and spoken as truth. The constant and unabated interpretation of law, the US Constitution, and the Holy Scripture has, for centuries, evolved into the bubbles of cultic thought that we endure today. Self-made theologians, government leaders, speculators, prophets, and politicians act as kings and priests self-perpetuating themselves with ideologies known only within their groupings.

The residue of the writer is left on his page. It is as indelible as any print.

Thought conceived and communicated as truth becomes 'the' truth for the purveyor, as well as, the inherent group. The bubble-effect eventually takes place within the traditions of thought with the group inside the bubble professing a manifesto of beliefs that are true to them, but not necessarily true to scripture, the law, or the

The Dissolution of Truth

constitution.

William Thomas and Dorothy S. Thomas, sociologists in the 1930's, theorem of reflexivity contends, "If people define things as real, they are real in their consequences". [1] It has also been stated that this theorem repeated says, 'the situations that men define as true, become true for them.[2] So it is within the religious realm as it is in the government and political realms, the man's perspective is true to him and that makes it the truth for him. What is stated is believed to be true, therefore it is speculated upon and acted upon as a fact particularly within the group that the statement is being perpetuated. The perpetuated speculation, or, revelation, is then delivered to the public as an offering of truth creating the personal dictum, "If it is true to me, then it is the truth."

Offense comes along this line to the lowest common denominator and that being the child. After all, is not what the battle is ultimately for...the mind of the child? Truth is left to the aristocracy of the people in charge and delivered as an edict for the loyal citizens to abrogate their responsibility to the realm of the unseen that being analytical thought. Voltaire stated, "The only way in which man can reason about objects is by his analysis. To begin straight from first principles belongs to God alone." [3]

The decimation of discernment is implied from the aristocracy of truth leaving the inbred truth supplanting itself as a substitutionary foundation of what truly is. Facts are no longer facts, but mere obstacles viewed as pariahs to the current philosophy or revelation of the day.

Hence, the propensity of the cult is for thought to be conceived in the mind of the leader, developed in cyclical unilateral interpretations, and then disseminated to the children no matter what their age. Cultic thought abounds today not only within the religious realm, but the geopolitical realm throughout our nation and world.

I believe the Holy Scripture to be wholly true. I state this with no apology. The fathers of our nation believed this to be true and often quoted from the scriptures as reference in their writings. There is, after all, only one Truth, the Word, found in Jesus Christ. We are admonished not to add to, or take away from that word. (Deuteronomy 12:32) However, it also states that, 'no prophecy of scripture is of any private interpretation, for prophecy never came by the will of man, but holy men of God spoke as they were moved by the Holy Spirit.' (2 Peter 1:20-21, NKJV)

Over the centuries, church leaders, as well as, many folk ignorant of what the Word of God actually says, have viewed this passage as a gateway to implied self-interpretation of the Word of God, becoming the incubator for misleading and false teaching to others and to the self. I call this "procreatic reflexivity" because of the constant seed producing effect that false teaching creates and incurs, over and over again. False teaching seeds itself in reflective thought and confession emanating from the leader to its populace, and the populace, goes and repeats the teaching. We have become a world of cults, religiously and politically, throughout every genre of leadership. Most men do not lead in truth; they lead by what they have been taught, their pride or the size of their wallet. The desire for the more propels the cultic leader to become the '. . . ever roaring lion, seeking whom he may devour.' (1 Peter 5:8, NKJV)

The astigmatism created in this layer of perceived truth into the retina of the hearer. The vision of the child is blurred unbeknownst to the child, but not all children, because many people believe what they want to believe as a result of former authorities, of whom they do not trust, rejections, or, just plain laziness. For decades now, these children have been told what to think and how to express what they are told. It is this astigmatism that keeps people from seeing what 'truly is'. This type of reflexivity thrives in the rejection of private study as it can only exist in the cultic thought of the group. Loyalty is demanded as analytical thought is submerged.

The truths men tell are believed to be innocuous and pithy, but as Thomas Paine discerned, there are men who speak from "Point-no-Point". [4] Men, whose values are only valuable to them, seeing gain, or, the next election, as the point and believing they bring no harm to the masses. After all, it is the masses that this group has enjoined to help in very particular ways with very particular personal motives.

The political and religious construct are analogous and are equally constituted in reflexive reciprocity. It is as though all men see what has been happening all along and have accepted these reflexive propensities as the social norm and in the eyes of the people, the leaders believe they are accepted, values and all. Nothing could be further from the Truth. Simply because men have cleverly gotten away with their menagerie of creations, they do not see that all they are are the sycophants of society living off of the populace they are enjoined to serve.

Reciprocity within the reflexive domain is a controlled substance made to benefit the leader. These leaders feed off of the ignorance of the masses who want to believe that good is in authority and that righteousness is not far off (Isaiah 46:13) Again, many people believe what they want to believe, that's why they give their money to the thieves in the financial district.

All we like sheep have gone astray; we have turned, every one, to his own way; And the Lord has laid on Him the iniquity of us all. (Isaiah 53:6, NKJV)

Sociopaths, disguised as political, religious, and financial leaders seek whom they may devour. How can we be purged from these afflictions when they, who are in authority over us, serve themselves as demagogues pursuing power, pleasuring themselves with self-indulgent refractorious personalities that bring new meaning to what is truly obstinate, stubborn and perverse.

I am undone.

Truth

Who knows the truth? Can anyone know it? Perhaps this is the avenue of my discontent. It seems in this day that the loudest person, or group, speaking is right, and all should listen. In the reflexive domain, people believe that a larger number of people constituting a majority gathering together determine rightness. If we examine the lack of analytical thought concerning these two current philosophies, we see how absurd the validity of the existence of these thoughts. To some, appearances are everything.

The homosexual community is an example of a group that has yelled the loudest for a seemingly long period of time. The group has joined together in agreement and has proved that their talking points to the right ears have been heard, hence, they have been getting their way for some years now. The political construct has listened. Hollywood, in both TV and movie creation, has listened and complied with the appearance that homosexuality is a commonplace way of life for a considerable number of Americans. The group has been able to come to America and demand that the definition of marriage be re-written. The power of this group is possessive to all and overwhelming to some.

The reflexive attributes within this group include the idea that if someone, or, some entity, does practically anything against their belief system, then that person or entity is presumed to 'hate' the group, or, someone in the group. Another attribute, positive in nature, is agreement. They are agreed that anyone in disagreement with them hates them and doesn't have the right to speak against them. They are agreed with the idea that they are 'born' homosexual.

I believe in the Word of God. The Word says that man was created in the image of God. The agreed belief of being 'born this way' would imply that God is homosexual, or could be. He is not, nor could he be. In Leviticus 18, the laws written were laws on sexual morality, who the people of God could not 'lie with' in a sexual way. There are 30 verses in that chapter with the majority of them being very specific with common sense in nature that you don't 'lie with' your uncle, cousin, aunt, mother-law, daughter-in-law, mother, father, nor anyone of any kin. You don't 'lie with' animals. Verse 22 is explicit, 'You shall not lie with a male as with a woman. It is an abomination.' (NKJV) God is faithful to Himself, God cannot lie as men and women are accustomed to doing.

If men are created in the image of God, they are created to be men and women are created to be women. The mere writing of this statement is comical to have to write it, but this is where we find the reflexive domain of the homosexual. The perspectives of this domain were created by themselves for themselves to perpetuate themselves onto the populace. They believe what they say about themselves including the word 'homosexual'. Who coined that term? Someone in the past coined a term to fit a belief system of ideas and behaviors and then perpetuated the belief that it was real and true. If I believe I am something that someone else has told me that I am does that make it so? Is it the truth? If I believe I am something that I have told myself that I am; does that make it so? Is it the truth or have I been led to believe a mere lie to satisfy an immoral desire?

The Dissolution of Truth

If I say that homosexuality is a choice, a lifestyle…that it is behavioral and nothing more…that is what I believe. Homosexuals believe that 'so called' protected rights of civility are claimed as theirs because a Divine Creator made them the way they are. However, anyone making a claim to be a homosexual, whether male, or female, has made a series of moral choices to behave in such a manner. This brings us to one of today's prevalent philosophies, 'Blame someone else for your decisions'. You cannot blame God if you fornicate and have sex with someone outside of marriage. You cannot blame God if you commit adultery by having sex with someone outside of the marriage bed if you are already married, or the partner is. You cannot blame God if you eat too much ice cream and fried chicken and have a heart attack. It would be your choice to do so.

This leads me to the point of having to acknowledge that for me to say that homosexuals are a part of the homosexual community would be errant. There is no such person who 'is' a homosexual. It is a lifestyle choice, not a sense of being. This also includes the transgender, who is not a different gender as they propose, they have simply chosen, as a result of emotional, spiritual and mental trauma to become something that they are not.

I am a male married to a female. Jesus said that if I look at a woman with lust in my heart, I have committed adultery with her, even though we did not touch. (Matthew 5:28) If adulterers gathered together and called themselves a group, common sense tells us what is in order and what is, and is not, natural. The rationale that if we can get the marriage definition re-defined from one man to one woman to a man with a man, or, a woman with a woman, then we can legitimately not be committing adultery and start having our tax benefits and insurance benefits kick in for our partners. Is this about truth, or, about the dollar and saving me money from additional taxes, or, paying additional insurance premiums? Here is where the area of equality is presumed by my re-defined definitions. The reflexivity attribute of mandatory re-defining of terms is obviously conclusive. If I live within a false domain, I have to have a world of re-defined terms created for me in order to live comfortably within my own order of existence.

This is merely an example of the fallacy of a person labeling another person and they believe they 'are'. Words are important. What we say to others about them is heard in the atmosphere and demonstrated in the flesh. Reflexivity thrives on this principle. One person believes something to be true and they tell another and get agreement. Agreement is power. It is a principle unto itself. Reflexive domains grow by the power of agreement, not loudness, largeness, or rightness.

The foundation of created philosophies and systems are based on complicated thought and continuance. Someone speaks a word, a phrase, a sentence, and, behold, creation takes place. Thoughts becoming words becoming belief systems are indeed systemic to all mankind, throughout all of time. Humanity prides itself in its thinkers. If that is the case, who thought up that a man sexually aroused by another man must 'be' a homosexual, therefore he 'is' a homosexual. This is to imply to our children that they can think as they choose, because they 'are'. It also implies that the children's thoughts are 'right in their own eyes'. In the order of nature, we know that this is not true. The truth of the matter is that if a man is sexually aroused by another man, he is thinking a thought that is antithetical to Biblical

The Dissolution of Truth

purity, is immoral, and is simply thinking towards exhibiting a lifestyle behavior that is a choice, a matter of freewill. The man is still a man who has chosen a particular way to live and nothing more. Someone told him he could that.

As Pilate asked Jesus, "What is truth?" (John 18:38, NKJV), the reader may be asking that as well. Jesus Christ declared Himself, "I am the way, the truth, and the life. No one comes to the Father except through Me." (John 14:6, NKJV). Here, the standard is clearly stated in the Word of God, that Jesus Christ Is the Truth. I believe this truth. I believe that the standard is in the Word of God. It is a non-deviating straight line.

Any concept, or philosophy, that does not abide in this truth would be considered a deviation. Truth has to be somewhere, it is in God Himself. He is faithful in His Word. The mind of man is the battleground for truth to be received, believed, and confessed.

Am I just another man purporting my own ideas of what truth truly is? Am I the sophomoric one? Does truth truly exist, and can we know for certain that truth truly does exist and come to know truth in our own mind and heart? Does truth change?

I cannot make another person believe what I believe, but I have come to the time in my life where the expression of the believed truth of the writer is mandatory. Truth does exist and does not change. I must express what I believe to be true. The wisdom of Solomon found in the Proverbs says,

"For my mouth will speak truth; wickedness is an abomination to my lips. All the words of my mouth are with righteousness; noth-

ing crooked, or perverse is in them. They are all plain to him who understands and right to those who find knowledge." (Proverbs 8: 7-9, NKJV)

"All scripture is given by the inspiration of God, and is profitable for doctrine, for reproof, for correction, for instruction in righteousness, that the man of God may be complete, thoroughly equipped for every good work." (2 Timothy 3:16-17, NKJV)

"But he who does the truth comes to the light, that his deeds may be clearly seen, that they have been done in God." (John 3:21, NKJV)

It is in my personal willingness to be examined by a power greater than myself that I find solace and rectitude. Most leaders, I have discovered, are challenged by examination and analysis. One may ask, "Who are you to challenge what someone says is the truth, or not, because in our current society, truth is primarily found in the eyes of the beholder and no one has the right to be the holder of all truth?" If that is the case, the Word of God is true again when it says,

"Every way of a man is right in his own eyes, but the Lord weighs the hearts." (Proverbs 21:2, NKJV)

Do not be caught equating a perspective with the Truth or a theory with a fact. There is only one absolute Truth and that Truth is found in Jesus Christ alone.

The Subversion of Truth

The evolution of thought expressed by many of today's political and religious leaders is as graduated lines emanating from an unknown source towards the absolute, rather than emanating from. The gradual force lines must come from the absolute, otherwise, the pervasive perversion of perception becomes the pernicious incarceration of the mind to only believe 'what I tell you and if you differ from what I say, you are unworthy'. Lies and perceptions demand autonomy, truth doesn't have to. Truth is. The refusal to tell the truth is blatantly celebrated within the domain.

Submission to authority is demanded in government as well as truth. Where there is no submission to the governing authorities, there is always the most definite probability of subjugation. Government demands to govern; it believes that it is its inherent right and domain. Truth is ultimate and will ultimately prevail over all governments.

In the season of evolution, truth is questioned and subverted. The multiplication of thought disguised as truth, or, even as facts, arises from the midst as vapor in the atmosphere. It is then transmogrified to fall as rain into the hearts and minds of men. Words spoken with authority like seeds sown by a sower are allowed to be sent into the atmosphere to change men's minds from what is supposed to be to what the leader has chosen it to be. Thought becomes reversed. What is not absolute becomes the believable.

Absolute truth makes no such demand of subjugation. Absolute truth is. It has not moved; it has not changed. It does not require defending. The transmogrified lines of perceptions and suppositions have splintered casting their wares towards the minds of the children with intolerance towards the absolute. The ONE absolute remains covered in layers of thoughts, words, and deeds confessed by the souls of men transfixed on themselves and the desire of the vapor.

Men, as directed by the seeds of the vapor, think thoughts of a new way, a new order; change from what is. But change to what? The seeds are planted in fertile soil, layered over and fertilized by the mortifying of the absolute. Man is momentarily fulfilled by facile frivolities of the mind offered up as the latest truth of the day delivered during free press conferences. "Not-a-leader" leaders lead the leaderless into eventual ditches of despair.

Reparations are incalculable as infinity is to stupidity for the problems created by the misled "not-a-leaders". These so-called leaders who choose to be misled by the divine providence of their minds characterize this season of time and we are the worse for it. I am admonished to pray for those in authority over me, God certainly knows best. This leads us to the purpose of indoctrination:

1) Proselytize the mind

2) Capture the mind

3) Churn the mind

4) Change the ideologies in the systems, beginning with the government to exude power over the educational system.

5) Train up the young adults to train up the children according to the pervasive ideology.

The Dissolution of Truth

Governmental, educational, and religious systems are not concrete. These systems are made up of and led by men and women with their own belief systems. Leaders teach teachers to teach ideology. People teach what they are and what they believe even though they might not ever teach it from a book. It is the ideologies, philosophies, and belief systems that rule the airwaves, the offices, the classrooms, and the pulpits. "Keep your heart with all diligence, for out of it spring the issues of life." (Proverbs 4:23, NKJV)

It is what is inside of man that heals, or kills, that unites, or divides. It is what is inside of a man to love, or to hate, to define, or to be misaligned. It is in the heart of men to believe any given philosophy and to create their own belief system according to the tenure of themselves in relation to their family, culture, education, and religious preferences. Everyone believes in something. These four: family, culture, education, and religion are all inputs and influences. Does the government have a right to rule these four areas of influence?

The lack of family creates a greater dependency on the other influences. Culture includes, but is not limited to: human interaction in the speaking, listening, and behavioral domain in the immediate and the intermediate peripheral human relationships. In our season of time, cultural relationships have increasingly become more important to the self and more influential to the self than the family when the family allows the culture rule over the home and, at times, the culture invades the home at the behest of someone in the home.

Most people desire to be a part of a group of like-minded people. The heart desires and will submit to the cultural like-minded philosophy that lies at the doorstep and knocks repeatedly to come in to the minds of our children through the media, entertainment, sports, and peer opportunity. The belief system of the given philosophy defines its own words. For example, militant Islamic philosophy today that says in order for me to prove my love for my god, I must hate the unbelievers. Love, then, is determined by my level of hate. Hate for others is love for my god. How well I hate is how well I love my god. I am true to my god by my faithfulness to my hating the infidels, who happens to be anyone who does not believe what I believe. This is the writer's understanding of the mind of the terrorist and what they interpret their writings to command.

This philosophy is resolute and believes it is absolute truth. Can there be more than one absolute truth? In my research, one dictionary had ten definitions of the word - absolute, which, seem to be congruous within the context and four multi-faceted definitions of truth. Another online source had twenty-eight philosophies, or, theories, of truth. (Wikipedia) It is no wonder that the thought of absolute truth would be relegated as another antiquated and ridiculous idea.

The mind of the child is proselytized everyday by what its family, or the lack of family, allows. Whatever comes into the home, or the classroom, goes into the mind of the child. Now, they are told what to think. The input does not vaporize, it is stored and churned as C.S. Lewis understood and wrote about in "The Abolition of Man".

Systems will do whatever is necessary to deliver their beliefs into the minds of the children. The variations of principles are dispersed throughout the varying streams of media, entertainment, and human interactions so that the diversity of America, seemingly one of its greatest attributes, will become its demise. The plethora of diversity in America, if left unchecked, will be its eventual downfall and submission to a more unified authority. What we are continuing to

The Dissolution of Truth

teach our children:

1) If you can learn to bounce, throw, or kick a ball better than anyone else, you can make millions of dollars. We make the players of children's sports and games gods in our nation. Here: Sports rules.

2) If you can sing, or dance better than the other person can sing, or dance, again, you can make millions of dollars. Here: Entertainment rules.

3) Do whatever you have to do to win. This is seen in all of life.

4) Give me your money and God will pay you back. This is the hyped preacher's ethics.

5) If I have large numbers of people following me, I am right and I am successful.

6) As long as I am sincere to what I believe, that's all that matters.

7) If I can lie to you about what is, or is not, and get away with it, then I can cheat you out of your money, play you for the fool, and blame you for it. This is the false prophet's game.

8) Hustling stolen goods is rewarded with money and notoriety whether the stolen goods are the possession of another by way of an object, a dollar, a life, or a love.

What are we teaching our children, or allowing our children to be vicariously taught by others?

Terry Lursen

The Power of Charismatic Personalities

Recognizing that it is God Who has first acknowledged the waywardness of man let us move on towards the exposure of the reflexive domains within the liberal minded political, religious, and financial constructs. Reflexivity breeds personal truth where ideology prevails over reality. Leaders entice simple minds with their ideologies, and are believable, not because of truth, facts, or reality, but most often because of imbued sentiment. Cultic leaders are attractive for many reasons. But why is this? Why are cultic leaders and their false promises and teachings so attractive? Is it their charismatic personalities; their perceived nobleness; their ever-increasing ideologies that seem to change with the tides every day…perhaps so, perhaps all.

But it is also within the heart of man to allow himself down a deceptive path for there must be a way out of his predicament; his conflict; his constant contradiction of what is and what ought to be. "The toiling masses, the immense majority of mankind who are suffering under the incessant, meaningless, and hopeless toil and privation in which their whole life is swallowed up, still find their keenest suffering in the glaring contrast between what is and what ought to be, according to all the beliefs held by themselves, and those who have brought them to that condition and keep them in it. . . The sufferings of the working classes, springing from the contradiction between what is and what ought to be, are increased tenfold by the envy and hatred engendered by their consciousness of it."[1]

The Dissolution of Truth

Man desires a deliverer, no matter what his class, or creed. He wants to believe that his leader's ideology is the truth and the true way for him to be set free from his conflict, poverty, and pain. Poverty comes not only in financial lack, but in educational, social, and moral decay. The ideology of the reflexive leader meets me at my pain and his words are soothing to my soul. His words become my truths and I am willing to serve his ideologies even though somewhere deep inside my conscious is telling me, 'this may be too good to be true'. I take a blinds eye to his exploitation of the people he is chosen to serve.

If there is any inkling to the pricking of the conscious wherein I find myself being sold on an ideal that is 'too good to be true', then it is what it is, too good to be true. It's time to walk away, but here is where the lack of discernment meets need and when need hears what it wants to hear, then need agrees with its ears and its ears are itching to hear.

This basic concept is so simple and yet it acts as a hook to catch many folk even still. The reason being is that there are always children growing into adolescents growing into young adults growing into influence and paychecks; or, in the domain, viewed as pawns that the sensuous leader can use for his own purposes. Oswald Chambers says to test your teachers. "There are two tests - one is the fruit of the life of the preacher, and the other is the fruit of the doctrine. The fruit of a man's life may be perfectly beautiful, and at the same time, he may be teaching a doctrine which, if logically worked out, would produce the devil's fruit in other lives. It is easy to be captivated by a beautiful life and to argue therefore what he teaches must be right. Jesus says, 'Be careful, test your teacher by his fruit.' The other side is just as true. A man may be teaching beautiful truths and have magnificent doctrine, while the fruit in his own life is rotten." [2]

We see this played out every day and every day we disregard the signs. If a leader decides to lead people in a way as to incite bigotry, racism, or violence, that leader is leading others to the devil's fruit. His fruit is his heart and his followers he is responsible for. Laws have been created to hold bar tenders and party holders accountable for the alcohol that their constituents consume so that they don't serve the drunk so much so as to enable the drunk to go out at night and kill someone with a vehicle. Inciting words are more important and have killed more people than alcohol ever could. Leaders will eventually be held accountable.

Jesus said, "Beware of false prophets, who come to you in sheep's clothing, but inward they are ravenous wolves. You will know them by their fruits. Do men gather grapes from thorn bushes, or figs from thistles? Even so, every good tree bears good fruit, but a bad tree bears bad fruit. A good tree cannot bear bad fruit, nor can a bad tree bear good fruit. Every tree that does not bear good fruit is cut down and thrown into the fire. Therefore by their fruits you shall know them." (Matthew 7:15-20, NKJV)

We are to test our teachers and leaders and our leaders have to be open and forthright enough to allow their fruit to be examined. This Jesus principle is not to create mistrust in our religious and political leaders. However, the examination must commence and continue as long as there is a leader and a follower. There must be a willingness to communicate specificity in honesty, integrity, and reality. Does my leader dwell in the propensity of light?

Solomon said,

Let us hear the conclusion of the whole matter:

Fear God and keep His commandments,

For this is man›s all.

For God will bring every work into judgment,

Including every secret thing,

Whether good, or evil.   (Ecclesiastes 12:13-14, NKJV)

Kings and Pawns

Pawn - 1. A chess piece of lowest value. 2. A person or an entity used to further the purposes of another. [1]

A pawn, in the social sense, is also known as a tool, instrument, toy, puppet, dupe, or a stooge. How does your leader view you?

The test of a leader can also be performed by asking a few simple questions that deserve honest answers:

What do you really think about your followers?

How do you feel about the people that follow what you have to say?

The discernment of pretense is often difficult. "Pious pretense, not hypocrisy (a hypocrite is one who tries to live a two-fold life of his own ends and succeeds), but a desperately sincere effort to be right when we know we are not." [2]

Pretenders and hypocrites are usually revealed in this life. It is of the most extreme difficulty to fool all of the people all of the time. How the leader truly regards his constituency is not commonly reflected in the immediate. New leaders breed new auras; new ideas; new concepts; adrenaline and dopamine. He knows this and is aware that he thinks he is somebody. There is absolutely nothing wrong with a leader with a specific calling, purpose, and destiny. But, does he believe that his followers have an equal calling, purpose, and destiny?

The Dissolution of Truth

Does the government leader realize his relationship to other men in the United States is based upon:

"...these truths to be self-evident: that all men are created equal; that they are endowed by their creator with inherent and inalienable rights; that among these are life, liberty, and the pursuit of happiness: that to secure these rights, governments are instituted among men, deriving their just powers from the consent of the governed; that whenever any form of government becomes destructive of these ends, it is the right of the people to alter or abolish it, and to institute new government, laying its foundation on such principles, and organizing its powers in such form, as to them shall seem most likely to effect their safety and happiness..." [3]

Does the leader believe that he is a man among men, or does he believe that he is a king among pawns? The propensity of the common man is recognized to himself, for, hopefully, he knows his lot, and his desire to change his stars. It was the case with the acknowledgement of Thomas Paine who declared equality among men when he stated, "Mankind being originally equals in the order of creation, the equality could only be destroyed by some subsequent circumstance; the distinctions of rich, and poor, may in great measure be accounted for, and that without having recourse to the harsh ill sounding names of oppression and avarice. Oppression is often the consequence, but seldom or never the means of riches; and though avarice will preserve a man from being necessitously poor, it generally makes him too timorous to be wealthy. But there is another and greater distinction for which no truly natural or religious reason can be assigned, and that is, the distinction of men into KINGS and SUBJECTS. Male and female are the distinctions of nature, good and bad the distinctions of heaven;

but how a race of men came into the world so exalted above the rest, and distinguished like some new species, is worth enquiring into and whether they are the means of happiness or misery to mankind." [4]

In the writing of the Declaration of Independence, this writer believes that when Thomas Jefferson penned that all men are created equal, he was referring to that of KINGS and SUBJECTS, not the plethora of ignorance that exudes itself amongst the populace today. The reflexive domain of the monarchy displays beliefs that exemplify man's perceived differences in kingship, lordship, noblemen, and commoners. These are all man created ideas by the 'heathen', as Mr. Paine expressed, not by God, as some believe, for the soul purpose of governing the way a chosen man chooses to govern. Men trying to live as kings make grave attempts to justify their internal beliefs that their followers are merely pawns sent to him to use for his own purposes. I see this in our nation today. Ideology is promoted over reality with facile expressions of cliché's and slogans being left as the order of things that are. These expressions are often repeated, repeatedly, and are used as talking points for the group and group enlistment.

The end all to this domain is eventual destruction. Revolt will eventually occur whether it takes place in the same generation, or, in the generations to follow. Revolt from inequality is imminent. If a man believes he is a king among pawns, he has created his own truth about himself and others that are under his care.

The lack of truth in any given relationship between two, or more, parties creates escalating mistrust leading to a proper level of distrust and expulsion of the connected heart. The Middle East is aflame from this disgust.

The Dissolution of Truth

If the reflexive domain is not built on truth and reality, then its foundation is built on the lesser than. Speculation, supposition of thought, generational loss, and the intimidating factor of the oppressed mind are typical building blocks of the domain's repose. When I do not have to tell the truth, then I can simply plant a seed thought and allow the thought to do its work.

Knowing that we reap what we sow, our words become the seeds of our future. The sower continues to reap what he sows and sows what he reaps. If the sower sows seeds of speculation in the marketplace, or the political spectrum, there is the great probability that what he says will come to fruition and then he can capitalize on the supposition of thought propagated by the media. The media is the wind, and it "blows where it blows"....the receptors are the proselytes' ears that are to carry the seeds of speculation to the mangers for their minds to feed off of until their hands give their wallets back to the sower.

Jesus said that we would always have the poor among us; we have the foolish with us as well. Could it be that Jesus was not specifically speaking of monetary poorness, but intellectual, spiritual and mental poorness as well? If I do not learn from my father, my teachers or my own teaching from reading the wisdom of the ages, then I am left to the device of the domain to be used and abused. We must teach our children well to avoid the generational losses of spiritual truth, education, financial management, the importance of the family, and what the true order of things are to be. If we do not teach our children well what we know explicitly to be true, the domain will gradually steal their hearts, minds, and wallets for the furtherance of its kingdom.

It is what we believe to be inconsequential that is destroying what we have always believed would be with us. If we do not love our spouses truly, then the domain knows what to give them in a time of need or of pain. If we believe our deepest beliefs to be inconsequential through the non-practice of our beliefs, our children will not make the transfer. Have your beliefs been transferred to your children? What do your children believe? The domain is waiting for them. Generational loss is gradual and deadly. The non-practice of the truths we hold dear are decaying keys to doors we need to keep open.

It is as though we say to our children, 'Go play in the ocean,' as we watch from the shore. We lie back on the sand in the debtors repose and close our eyes to rest a bit from our responsibilities while our children step further out into the waves and the currents that they do not perceive is waiting for them. They wade further out trying to swim, just having fun, just having fun. Little do they know, the riptide is beneath and is stronger than the mightiest of the strong. 'If I just swim with the riptide, I can swim out of it,' they think as they have been taught. They struggle and become frightened. It is their fear and the fear of the tide and its strength that pulls them under. Swim wide and not against, remove and swim wide. Swim with the tide and remove so slowly what you have so quickly enjoined.

Some are lost in the riptide of inconsequentially. Some make it back, never to venture in the water again. What we believe to be inconsequential will have its reckoning day. You must spend time with your children and teach them well. You must stop spending money. . .

Our times are not inconsequential. What our Father has placed us here has a purpose and a meaning. Find out what that is and do not let it go. What you have been given is life. Live it! And do not allow the domain to dominate your mind or the minds of your children. Find

The Dissolution of Truth

out what truth is and live in that truth.

My inaction towards what I believe to be inconsequential leads me to busy myself with the things of the day that I believe that are of consequence and that I must put my hands to. This is how most of us live our lives. We do what we feel is necessary, whether we want to do it, or not. This may include going to work, cleaning our home, paying our bills, taking care of our lawn, spending time with our families, spending time alone with God, and so on. We Americans have things to do. The majority of us educate ourselves through schooling and through personal care, but we cannot know all things at all times, that is impossible. We rely on teachers, preachers, counselors, friends, and media of all sorts, to tell us what is necessary for the day's news and education.

Because we cannot know all things at all times, the trust that we put into our government leaders, our religious leaders, and the media to tell us the truth about our local, state, and national circumstances is for certain changing, but we still want to trust people in the expectation of them telling us the truth.

If we do not educate ourselves with relative knowledge, we really do not know if our leader is telling us the truth. When is the last time we read the Bible? When is the last time we read, and had a clear understanding of the Constitution of the United States? Have we ever read the constitution? Have we ever read the Declaration of Independence, or, have we relied upon others to tell us their version of these documents? Have we ever read a book by one of the framers of our nation and read what they meant by their writings? Have we educated ourselves so that we can have a valued conversation with another person regarding these documents, or do we simply talk about what we have been told by a leader, or the media, what these documents say?

My belief about the inconsequential things is almost as dangerous as ignorance. Ignorance regarding these documents is as plentiful as sand. Those who believe they have the educated, upper hand have the knowledge, or, are supposed to have the knowledge to teach the masses. It is supposed to be inherent for a teacher/leader to speak the truth about what is concerning any of these documents in order to relay a proper foundation for Americans to move in. This needs to be a conversation, rather than an arrogant indoctrination. How do I know what you say is true? The leader with the greater knowledge is susceptible to either telling the truth, or, becoming an uncommon force by his persuasive manipulation of the truth. In this instance, the greater knowledge may, or, may not contain truth, for its relativism to the things of the day will force its existence onto the ignorant.

Those ignorant to uncommon forces will be subjected to the things of the day. Ignorance has nothing to do with race. The relativistic uncommon force will propagate its views on a divided foe. The power of agreement rules supremely.

The reward of agreement is granted to the loyal. Loyalty to the agreed upon transcends factual truth. Thus the agreed upon ideology becomes the relative truth of the day. An example of this is when a President tells his people that the Supreme Court does not have the authority to overturn a law. He knows what he is saying is not true, but do others that he is speaking to know that? Hence personal perception becomes reality, therefore whatever is real, must be true.

The Dissolution of Truth

In the case of uncommon forces, many people believe 'my personal perception equals truth...'my truth'.

"Then Jesus said to those Jews who believed Him, 'If you abide in My Word, you are My disciples indeed. And you shall know the truth and the truth shall make you free.'" *(John 8:31-32, NKJV)*

I have often heard the love of God interpreted according to personal perception along with the idea that the person is set free by truth... this, usually being relegated to 'any' truth. There is quite an internal emotional impact exhibited when a person believes something to be true, accepts it as fact, and then confesses the 'believed truth' as fact.

If I believe as the antinomian, that faith alone is necessary to salvation and that I am not bound by any further moral law, then I stop short of the whole truth of the Gospel of Jesus, for He also said, "Therefore if the Son makes you free, you shall be free indeed." (John 8:36, NKJV). My freedom comes by being 'in' Him, not outside of Him. My freedom comes from abiding 'in' His Word. Abiding in Him is how I know truth, the whole truth.

The antinomian effect transcends our culture today when a perceived homosexual can believe that he has salvation in Christ, and yet permitted, according to his own belief system, to be free from any moral law that would be fundamental to the absolute truth of the Gospel of Jesus Christ. He, then, becomes agreed with like others who believe as he believes and considers himself right because he has created his own truth but is actually exhibiting a lack of knowledge of the whole counsel of God.

There is an afterlife where men will be judged according to their beliefs and what they have taught others to believe. The propagation of beliefs to the less knowledgeable is supremely great in the eyes of God. We will be held accountable for what we teach ourselves, our families, and others to believe, and, if followed by agreement with others, we will either celebrate in jubilation, or, suffer the consequences in eternity for these beliefs. I would pray that all would celebrate, but, I know that that is not to be the case.

It is past time to carefully examine what we agree to and it is past time to take seriously what we teach others to believe for there is a millstone waiting for the accursed who teach others offenses to the Word of the Lord and to His children.

The Value of Truth

The occurrence of knowing a thing is relative to the perspective of the knower in its journey to seek the truth in a matter. Not all things are revealed at times and our tendency is to believe what we see as a permanent matter, yet permanency is just as reliable as our perceptions of truth. We are floating in a river of space and time and the truth that we think we have been told is as fleeting as the air that we just expelled.

If I am a citizen in a community that delves into the dubious, did the dubious derive itself from itself or has it always been? Duplicity is the order of the day delving into synchronicity. The atmosphere requires it of itself for the current ideas of duplicity multiply at a seemingly rapid pace in order for the hearer to hear what it hears and have it reinforced over and over again.

What is it that hears, or sees? Do you actually believe your eyes, your ears? How is it that you have come to know a thing when you don't even realize that the dubious has winked at you and you think you are friends?

How is it that one arrives at truth in a world where the dubious and the duplicitous mangle principles of truth with their version of a controlled substance called a word. Definitions are re-arranged to suit the manner of the day. It is in the atmosphere where they are grasped, inculcated and churned into philosophies that have been around since the days of Sodom. There is no permanent matter in truth, so the loudest and the largest part the waters for they are the lords of the manor, for today.

There is, after all, only one spiritual Truth, and all other truth as we may know it derives from this single Holy Truth. Any other thing, word, principle or idea that is not of this very particular spiritual Truth is a flow from another source. We humans have the tendency to find others quite remarkable when they are simply being themselves, when in actuality, what we should find remarkable is that we can see where there is no truth in their being or their emanations. Shakespeare is often misquoted with his character saying, "To thine own self be true" for he was speaking from the antithesis of the knowing for the lie had had its way.

Can you really know a thing, a person? Does anyone truly know you like you know you? Do you know yourself in truth or do you know yourself as you think you know you or hope that you are but are as self-deceived as the deceiver himself? Knowing the truth in a matter is not a fine art nor is it a matter of quintessential knowledge. Knowing truth is a spiritual matter, a Holy Spiritual matter at that.

The value of truth cannot be derived from a book, a sale, a pleasant smile, a popular teacher or the most secret of secrets. The value of truth is in a name and in a person. I am only known as the Master of Truth knows me and I can only know Truth as it is revealed to me. All other is anathema, including my right to myself and my own self-worth.

Truth knows me, but do I and can I know Truth as Truth knows my innermost parts? I will be known by others as they believe they think they know me, but I am known by Truth as I truly am whether

The Dissolution of Truth

I understand the truth about me as Truth understands me. If I realize that I truly do not know the truth about me as Truth knows me, can I ever know the truth of another human being without the revelation of the Master of Truth? I cannot form a righteous judgment of another for I am not Truth myself. I cannot take that which is not mine to take.

The value of Truth lies in the Master of Truth. Only He knows the Way, the Truth and the Life. I must know Him and in knowing Him, I am coming to realize that in me dwells no good thing, save Him and Him alone. It is in Him I find Truth in His innermost parts. Here and here. The Kingdom of God dwells within and it is only within His Spirit that the value of Truth is revealed.

Terry Lursen

The Importunity of a Lie

After thoroughly discussing truth in earlier writings in, we've now come to what causes all of this to be expedient in making matters clear and concise and that is the propensity of the lie and how perspective can entertain the lie and weave it into its substance in order that the said perspective then becomes substantiated on an inherent belief system that holds absolutely no value as it relates to truth. There is absolute Truth found in Jesus Christ for it is in Him that the path to true holiness exists. There is no stain in holiness and there is none holy like our God.

Importunity is that which begs to be heard and implanted in such a way that the unnatural becomes the natural and replaces that which can actually be defined as a fact with a perspective that is altered by the lie itself. The construct of the lie has intent and its intent is always to destroy truth whether one's perspective be made up of analyzed and critical data or is made of refined perspective that is derived over time inculcating facts that prove the existence of the perspective within the domain of truth. Truth is and can be maintained, however, the depravity of man almost always relinquishes itself to a lower road for the sake of compatibility and desire to match perspectives with the internal belief system born from anguish rather than peace and has the suggestion that peace is greater than truth.

The lie is subversive in tactic and replaces confidence with doubt, faithfulness with duplicity and dishonors unity and agreement with

The Dissolution of Truth

disharmony. If there is a smidgen of a lie mixed with a fact, it has the ability to persuade the most enabled intellectual into believing a terse and benign conclusion that is so far off base from the truth, that it eventually corrupts all in its path.

The evidence is clear that the usage of the lie in social, political and spiritual domains has had its place since the morning of time and throughout antiquity. It is the proverbial mind bending insertion of a doubt, "Did he really say?" Or, the lie can completely subvert by inserting a word or two or leaving out a word or two within an aforementioned fact in order to make a clear delineation from the real truth or factual content.

What is it about humans that it befalls them to believe the lie? Is it the depravity of man? The reminders from Isaiah, the Prophet and Paul, the Apostle, who stated that there is none righteous, no, not one, clearly open the door to the culpability of man to openly and unreservedly receive the lie for the importunity not only breathes within the heart of the lie, the importunity resides in the heart of man to desire that which he desires and needs to form some type of agreement with its belief system. It is, after all, the heart of a man and woman to receive the lie and join themselves to it that is most reckless and contentious with truth.

The importunity, then, lies within the domain of itself completely outside the domain of truth and factual submission. When the depravity of man reaches into the atmosphere for its belief to be substantiated, the lie that has been created, then has a host to join itself to. Both the lie and the host have been and continue to search for each other making both importunistic in the persistent and insistent demand to be heard and agreed with.

It is, however, not the lie that will be held accountable in the day of judgment, but the purveyor of the lie that will be held completely accountable for every idle word.

If you happen to care at all about your future or the future of your children, get to know the truth and receive the Holy Spirit of Truth that convicts the world of its sin, of judgment and of righteousness. Jesus said that He is the Way, the Truth and the Life and that no man can come to the Father except through Him. Examine your own heart and allow Him to examine even further where your own depravity refuses to allow you to go and see what lies in the depths of your heart that makes you want to believe a lie whether it be shared by a man, a woman or a spirit. If you choose to believe a lie, the importunity of it will cause you to share it. Believe what you will for your eternal destination depends on truth and the agreement of it within your heart as well as the hearts of your children.

The Dissolution of Truth

The Power of Perspective

"It is our needs that interpret the world; our drives and their For and Against. Every drive is a kind of lust to rule; each one has its perspective that it would like to compel all the other drives to accept as a norm." [1]

Nietzsche goes on to say, "Against positivism, which halts at phenomena - 'There are only facts' - I would say: No, facts is precisely what there is not, only interpretations. We cannot establish any fact "in itself": perhaps it is folly to want to do such a thing." [2]

Because a man such as Neitzsche thought these thoughts does it make them true? Are these thoughts, which happen to have been translated through time from the mind of the perverse to his future readers, the dwelling place of the reflexive domain?

"It is in the accusatory state that we deem our brothers and sisters in prejudice. For to deal in prejudice is to deal a judgment without entertaining all of the evidence - the facts. If there are no facts, only interpretations, then, the law will side with the best interpreter. "'Everything is subjective,' you say; but even this is interpretation. The 'subject' is not something given, it is something added and invented and projected behind what there is. - Finally, is it necessary to posit an interpreter behind the interpretation? Even this is invention, hypothesis." [3]

Are any humans capable of knowing truth? If truth is things as they really are, albeit the 'reality', are any of us capable of re-telling reality to our neighbor without prejudice? Is it possible to purview the totality of a truth from our perspective of the world? Do we realize our lot, our position, in life?

Do we realize our predilections? The majority of us dwell in vast predilection. We come to each other with our ideas as congealed salad. It is premade with our favorite ingredients and set to jell in the refrigerator. We, then, present it to our 'guests' as a concoction that they are to sit down and eat, not realizing and not caring that the ingredients are repulsive to the guests. Our words are morsels to the ears, to the hearts of mankind, and have become tainted as meat turns after days of sitting.

If I desire for someone to listen to me, what does that say of myself? Who are you, oh man, that anyone should listen to what you have to say? Is your truth consummate of reality? Or, are the listeners getting a strange concoction of perspective and interpretation of what one man has seen and relating? Is it possible for the listener to hear without self-interpretation? Do you expect your listeners to think while you speak? Is there any relative knowledge at work in the sound waves coming from your breath?

Honestly, I have a hard time growing grass in my yard at home. By the time summer rolls around I see that I can't even grow grass right. My neighbors seem to be able to. However, they use a tremendous amount of fertilizer on their lawns. They really pile on the fertilizer and the more they pile it on, the greener the grass gets. Whether it is embellishment, or manure, in the eyes of God, it is all the same. Truth does not need embellishment, perspective relishes in it.

The Dissolution of Truth

Have the best tort lawyers become our legislators? Do we believe what we believe as a result of investigation and education, or, do we simply believe what we are told? The undereducated are morsels to the demagogue.

dissolution - the act or process of dissolving: as

a: separation into component parts

b: 1) decay, disintegration. 2) death

c: termination or destruction by breaking down, disrupting, or dispersing

d: the dissolving of an assembly or organization

e: liquefaction [4]

truth - 'Whatever you say it is'.

Who, or, what, is behind this dissolution of truth? Are our leaders, our Presidents, Senators and Congresspersons merely pawns?

Terry Lursen

Change

My son, Stephen, took me to a garden on the college campus where he had completed his undergraduate work in art and oil painting. In the garden, he showed me a pagoda that he had painted a painting of a few years ago. I immediately recognized the structure because the oil painting rests on a wall in the breakfast area in our home.

As I observed the painting again this morning, I was enlightened by my son's viewpoint at the time of the painting. The garden, at the time, was young as was the brush. The plants and the greenery surrounding the pagoda were short in stature, being that a lot of the growth was new. Thus was the vantage point of a young artist in training. His eyes saw newness, clean lines, and a strong structure.

As he took me along the trails of the garden, though, he showed me, the current view of the pagoda from the original vantage point. His first observance was of the plants and the greenery having had grown up along the trail obscuring the view of the pagoda. We stood where he had stood those few years back to get the view from the same vantage point at the time of the painting. I could easily make out the roof of the structure and only a bit of the right side. The garden had matured and, actually, we could not see the structure from the old vantage point.

Although the eyes of the painter have matured, the garden had done so as well. Time is irrevocable. This is real and natural change.

Social Liberalism

It is in the recognition of growth and change that we become more at ease with life as we know it. There are many aspects of life that are common to all men in their knowing of mankind and of nature, however, the more specific one gets into the knowing of mankind and nature, the less common the knowledge known to all. Common knowledge and common sense are truly not so common anymore mainly as a result of the diversity of belief systems, along with the advancements in science and technology, that have been integrated into our American society. What is common, or, common sense, to me is not so common to a man with a completely different and diverse cultural background. The adverse is also true, what is common to another man, may, or may not be, common to me. The knowledge of mankind works that way in culture and in environment.

However, does the structure of the common change to drastically in nature? Life and growth, change and death occurs to us all. It is in the order of nature that there are commonalities of thought and being that we all know things as they are, or, ought to be. It is in this order of nature and of things that tells us in our conscience that life is good, or, supposed to be, and that violence and murder are wrong. It should not be easy, or common, to kill another human being, any more so than it is to strike another with a fist. Anger is common to us all, but our response to anger is not so common.

The need for food, clothing, and shelter is common to us all, but how we obtain these basic necessities is not common, save that of work, and even that is not common anymore. Diverse belief systems have changed commonalities at the root of mankind and even at the root of nature. It is what a man believes that guides his life and, as a leader, what guides his home, his community, and his nation. If he believes that the provision of food, clothing, and shelter should come from the work of his hands, or his mind, then that has been as common to man since the garden of Eden. If another man believes that his provision for food, clothing, and shelter should come at the expense of another without any use of his hands, or mind, that being work; then he believes that he has a providential right to take from the one who has and give it to himself or give it to another one in need who also refuses to work. This is the commonplace sense of the thief, the slothful, and the liberal.

"But we command you, brethren, in the name of our Lord Jesus Christ that you withdraw from every brother who walks disorderly and not according to the tradition which he received from us. For you yourselves know how you ought to follow us, for we were not disorderly among you; nor did we eat any one's bread free of charge, but worked with labor and toil night and day, that we might not be a burden to any of you, not because we do not have authority, but to make ourselves an example of how you should follow us. For even when we were with you, we commanded you this: If anyone will not work, neither shall he eat." (2 Thessalonians 3:6-10, NKJV)

Nature tells us that the man who did not work for his gain does not understand the value of the gain, nor does he understand the value of the expense that someone else paid for that gain. Gain does not simply materialize as some preach, but comes at the expense of another. It is the ebb and flow of capitalism, socialism, communism,

The Dissolution of Truth

and thievery.

If a man has obtained a leadership position and the ensuing power that comes along with it and yet, has not paid the price through work, sacrifice, and experience, or gained the knowledge and wisdom required regarding that leadership position, that man does not understand the value of his position and will rule unjustly and ignorantly as a result. Truly, there are rank amateurs in all walks of life in leadership over us.

It is these inane leaders who, seemingly, have attained much with little, or, no effort, that espouse their belief systems onto their masses. If one believes that he does not have to work for what he has been given, he will teach others to do the same. If I believed that, then, it would only seem right that my kind should be as I am only to the extent that everyone should be equal, but not equal to me because, after all, I am their leader and they owe me for the gain that I have taken from others and given it to them so that everyone is equal, except me, of course, because I am their leader and I continue to take from others to make the others equal and the others give to me more power and more gain that I can disperse because I am the leader and I know how to take from others to make all equal, except me, of course, I just get rich.

This is the cause of the social liberalist. Strangely enough, however, the social liberalist believes that this is the cause of the capitalist. The view of the liberalist is skewed and obscured, though, because he has not seen the creation, growth, and change as the effects of work, but, rather sees prosperity and success as an opportunity to take from the rich and give to the poor at the expense of the creator/worker. The social liberalist is the opportunist who sees the blessing of a creator, calls it his own, and, then disperses it to others for his own personal gain.

In nature, this is known as theft, nothing more and nothing less. God has shown us Himself that the child of a monarch has no place on the seat of a throne.

"But it is not so much the absurdity as the evil of hereditary succession which concerns mankind. Did it ensure a race of good and wise men it would have the seal of divine authority, but it opens a door to the FOOLISH, the WICKED, and the IMPROPER, it hath in it the nature of oppression. Men who look upon themselves born to reign, and others to obey, soon grow insolent; selected from the rest of mankind their minds are early poisoned by importance; and the world they act in differs materially from the world at large, that they have but little opportunity of knowing its true interests, and when they succeed to the government are frequently the most ignorant and unfit of any throughout the dominions." [1]

The social liberalist presumes the right of leadership as divine just as the son of a monarch presumes himself upon a throne.

"...Perception is common to everyone, so it is easy and in no way a mark of wisdom. Further, with regard to every science, we think a man wiser the more accurate he is and the more he can tell us about causes. Then, among the sciences, we hold one that is desirable for its own sake and for the sake of knowledge to be more truly wisdom than one that is desirable only for what follows from it, and the one that involves the giving of directions as more so than any that is subordinate to it; for the wise man ought not to be given instructions, he ought to give them, and he ought not to obey anyone else, someone less wise than he should obey him." [2]

And so it is in the obverse side of nature and the true order of things we see children leading parents and children becoming leaders in our communities, our churches, and in our government. How unfortunate we are.

"**When the righteous are in authority, the people rejoice; but when a wicked man rules, the people groan.**" (Proverbs 29:2, NKJV)

Terry Lursen

Defying Ubiquity

"We have the idea that God has only to do with the spiritual, and if the devil can succeed in keeping us with that idea, he will have a great deal of his own way; but Paul pushes the battle-line into every domain - "whatsoever things are honest...think on these things, " because behind them all is God." [1]

Why is it that that we are not told the Truth? The world wants to keep religion in a box for a number of reasons. Religionists believe that God is kept in a sanctuary and it is there that the masses should go and worship Him. Whether a true Christian believes this, or not, has become irrelevant, it has been and has increasingly become the behavior regardless of the belief.

If the so-called Christians go to worship their God in the church, the sanctuary, the chapel, the hall, the place...then they go to the box and leave Him there in the box so that they can get on with the rest of their lives. Is this a perception, or, reality? Is this type of behavior the true belief of the Christian, or is it only what is seen from the outside? Why is there an 'outside'?

There is definitely an 'outside' to the Christian life, I have seen it, and lived it. It is the lifestyle of the one who does not clearly understand the omnipresence of an omnipresent God. If the Christian does not understand the Jesus Who said, 'I will never leave you, not forsake you...', then it would seem that that Christian could perceivably

The Dissolution of Truth

leave God where he last worshipped Him.

It is through the teaching of the church leaders and through the living out of the teachings of the Christians that non-believers have seen with their own eyes that God is 'at church' because this 'guy doesn't act like Jesus', or, 'God is love and this guy is not loving', or, 'this guy is worse off than I am, why do I need to go and listen to that stuff?'

There are a myriad of thousands of sights and sounds that non-believers have seen of us, the ones that call themselves Christians here in America, and they have heard with their own ears and seen with their own eyes that 'this thing doesn't work because I don't see anything different, except the possibility of spewing hatred where I thought there was to be love'.

It is what the spirit of religion has done to the church, that is...go to the box, give your worship and money there, leave, and we hope to see you next week, or next Easter. If there is a Christian who would like to deny that this occurs, please continue to live in denial at your children's demise.

After all, once again, it is the heart of the children that the adversary desires, nothing more, nothing less.

This is what I have to say to the Christian church:

We are not one because the love of God is not shed abroad in our hearts. We are separate out of choice and convenience, not culture. There is no holy love in choice and convenience. Those have to do with what we want rather than what He wants. He, Jesus, learned obedience through suffering. He first loved and He first gave. Though

He was God in the flesh, He submitted to earthly authority.

As long as the word of God is taught, the people will listen and walk in it. When the traditions of men are taught, the people begin to have a doubt. The doubt raises questions, and the questions go unasked and unanswered resulting in mistrust. 'I don't really have a reason not to trust, but because I don't get to ask my questions, or, get the answers that I expect and understand, I am led by my doubt rather than the Truth'. There is no unity in doubt. Hence, there is no real holy love.

Perhaps the reason why we do not have unity in Holy Love is that we do not believe the same thing. The diversity in the church is the derision of the adversary. There is the power of an Almighty God in unity and agreement. Yesterday's and today's church has chosen the lesser, more convenient perceived road to tranquility...the road of tradition.

Someone on the outside, an example would be the reflexive domain of the homosexual, looks at that road and knows that he has seen that road before and laughs. They come together and unify in whatever the belief of the day is and construct a road of their own. Their road is being built and advancing in agreement, unity, and derision while the Christians pity themselves for being persecuted. Self-pity is a most egregious thing before an Almighty God.

The antichrist spirit looks at the church and says to 'keep your God in the box'. They defy ubiquity. They have not seen the omnipresent God in the flesh, of late, and teach so that their ideas become ubiquitous, rather than the Truth. The spirit of condemnation they have seen in us, and as a result, have turned that spirit back on us.

The Dissolution of Truth

God Is. God will prevail. It is through the Christians of today that He will use. Wake up! Teach what is pure, what is right, what is holy to your children, teach your children well. Cover them in loving prayer today.

Terry Lursen

Speaking in Truth on Marriage

Is truth in variation, truth, or is it only senses, appearances, and perceptions?

To speak on that which is true, or to speak on that which you perceive to be true, is to speak from your personal inclination to that which you believe to be true, or, hope to be true. To speak from truth is to speak from authority is to speak from a judgment seat. One's personal inclination, otherwise known as an opinion, is arbitrarily viewed, by the person speaking, as something far greater than it is in reality.

If you believe that what you say is true, it is true for you in that moment; is it therefore the truth because you say it is?

If someone speaks from truth, one speaks from a position of authority; does what you have to say speak from the weightiness of that position when you declare a thing about someone's health, for example, even though you are not his doctor? If you are not his doctor and you speak that which you believe to be true regarding his health, are you speaking life, or death, into the ears of the one whose health you have made yourself the authority over?

Aristotle arrived at the following conclusion: "If, then, it is impossible truthfully to assert and to deny anything at the same time, it is also impossible for contraries to belong to anything at the same time;

The Dissolution of Truth

either both must belong to it only in a way, or one must belong to it in a way, and the other absolutely."[1]

Through his proof development he argued his case to this conclusion. And, if it is true that two contraries cannot belong to anything at the same time, how can one speak truth when one vacillates between the ideal and the real?

If your presentation of the ideal is delivered as reality in truth, then what you are speaking is only what you hope to be true, but not true at all. Do you understand with the intellect that there is truth and that there is falsehood?

"...it is not possible, either, for there to be any intermediate between contradictory assertions; any one thing must be either asserted or denied of any other. This will become clear if we first of all define truth and falsehood. To say that what is is not, or that what is not is, is false, and to say that what is is, or that what is not is not, is true; so that the man who says that anything either is or is not will be speaking either truly or falsely; but where there is an intermediate assertion, neither what is nor what is not is being said either to be or not to be." [2]

Aristotle goes on to say that in order for one to hold a view regarding these things, we must start with a definition and the definition will fit the name, or term, of that which we speak.

If there is a known definition of truth, and a known definition of falsehood, but you do not hold to the asserted definitions, but create your own definition(s) to those terms, or any other terms, there is, therefore the impossibility of argument between the two sides of an opinion, because you have changed the basic foundation of the naming of terms by your re-writing of the definition(s) by your prescribed views.

In this case, your ideal is perceived real by your classification of your re-defined terms and statements. It then becomes implausible to argue the points because what is is not and what is not is.

This is, perhaps, an explanation of why the reflexive domain of the insurgent and the cult is complimented by its loudness and its largeness, because the ideal dwells in the perception of truth and can make of itself whatever it says it is, whether it is, or is not.

By creating new definitions for terms, such as truth, falsehood, or marriage, the reflexive domain removes the foundation of what is with the flow of change.

Truth is and must remain in a stated foundation of definition just as marriage is and must remain constant rather than having change as the authority in lieu of truth. Perceptions are perceptions and are as a river, ever changing. Truth is what is and is found in Jesus Christ. Marriage is the bond between one man and one woman. It is. It has always been, and will always be.

Led By Convictions

When in the course of human events we find ourselves being offended by others, it has been brought to my attention that offense is two-fold, the one being offended by the striking of their internal beliefs by another and the offender, who has presupposed their belief system onto the other. This is not the totality of being offensive, or of taking offense, but it is the due course of this discussion.

The angst that occurs through offense can be over in a moment, or it can create catastrophic and debilitating stress on the internal parts of the offended and for some, last forever due to unforgiveness. The internal stresses from being offended are also related to the level of maturity that one possesses. Some folk, who have absolutely no care whatsoever about what other people think about their opinions are oblivious to the common care and sense of decency regarding another's feelings, or thoughts. On the other hand, we still have some folk who live to be offended at just about anything because they dwell from anywhere to self-pity to wearing every bit of their emotion on their sleeves.

This does, however, bring us to our own personal convictions, how we relate those convictions, and how we respond when someone else does the same. If you believe what I believe, then most convictions shared become agreed upon and readily accepted, with the exception of a few nuances, all can be well between the two shared beliefs.

If you do not believe in the same things I believe in, then when one of us shares their convictions, there is this angst that begins to rise within us that, depending on how deep the differences are in the belief system, the anxiety can roll into frustration or anger in moments.

Thus our convictions and the sharing of the same are important, not only to us, but to the ones we share them with. They are important, because this is how we discover our commonality of beliefs with another, and conversely begin to see where others are in their beliefs and just how strongly they believe them.

It is in offense that drives many to the threshold of destructive anxiety and anger over the sharing of convictions as it also drives people in these United States to the voting booth. We need to know what our leaders believe whether we want to hear it, or not.

I find myself so terribly offended by our current (2008-2016) President and our Vice-President by their convictions, but why should I be offended, it is after all, what the liberal agenda believes and it is the liberal agenda they live and profess every day.

But here? Here in America? Why speak this now, after all the years of placating the public with their fluctuating opinions; why now, who does it serve to make a stance on homosexuality and homosexual marriage now?

If I have personally believed that 'my time is now to speak up and say something, say what I believe, and that this is my opportunity to speak...', then certainly it is everyone else's time as well, equality

The Dissolution of Truth

seems to be the timely notion. But what is it about what their beliefs that have me so compelled to stand up and say 'NO' to what they have to say?

I would tend to think that it is how deeply their beliefs go with me, to the core of Truth, I presume, because I have been taught that sex outside of marriage is a sin, and that a male having sex with another male is a sin and that a female having sex with another female is a sin. It is not the natural order of things. It is the foundation of immorality. Otherwise, there is no morality if there is no morality. The foundational set of beliefs and principles in morality include, do they not, a guard against sexual sins. If one is able to change the foundation of a thing, doesn't that change the make-up of the building you have erected? If you pull a building block from the foundation, what will be the end result of what you have built?

And so it is that the leaders of 300,000,000 people have professed their convictions to their populace because they are of a social liberal or socialist conception. "A man with a socialist conception of life cannot resist. The aim of his life is his personal welfare. It is better for his personal welfare for him to submit, and he submits." [1] The man in this belief system has to submit to the system, just as I attempt to submit to the One that I profess as my Lord.

But we are talking about our president and vice-president, aren't we? Are they so lowly as to submit to the exasperating liberal agenda, or are they the leaders of it? I believe that I am confused because the president should be the leader, but he did 'bat last in the line-up' when it came to professing beliefs. And, most problematic of all is that it seemed to me that the president of the United States was the leader of the nation and not specifically just the leader of the people of his beliefs. His level of respect for his office is not as deep as his predecessor.

Could real change be coming? If real change does not occur, the changes in our nation that President Obama professes will continue to take all of us on the road to his own personal convictions.

One of the stark differences in politics these days, and that, being a stark difference between a Democrat politician and a Republican politician is convictions. The convictions of a liberal Democrat are stated and unabated and that politician will serve the people in his/her constituency that voted for him/her, not everyone in the constituency, mind you; they serve the mutual belief system of their voting ideologues. They shake the hand that pats them on the back and the good-hearted Republican folk whine about the cronyism and the nepotism. These liberal Democrat folk can't help themselves, they do what they do and don't care what anybody thinks, particularly when it comes to murdering unborn babies. The vacillating Republican politician, however, is far different than his/her counterpart in their convictions, if they have any, at all. The vacillating Republican will pretend he/she knows what they're doing and act like the engaged listener to all things pertinent to their constituency and then go and do what the loudest, or the closest, person, or group has stated to do. Vacillators are without convictions and disregard those who voted for them. Their hands do not shake for friends, their hands shake for fear of losing their coveted jobs and so they ingratiate themselves across the aisle, getting punked all the way to the ballot box, waiting for a hand-out, once again, from people who do have convictions, such as, God, life, and righteousness.

Who Instituted Marriage?

Matthew 19:4-6 says, "And He answered and said to them, Have you not read that He who made them at the beginning 'made them male and female, 'And said, "For this reason a man shall leave his father and mother and be joined to his wife, and the two shall become one flesh'? "So then, they are no longer two but one flesh, therefore what God has joined together, let not man separate."

Malachi 2:13-17 says, "And this is the second thing you do: You cover the altar of the Lord with tears, with weeping and crying; So He does not regard the offering anymore, nor receive it with goodwill from your hands. Yet you say, "For what reason?" Because the Lord has been witness between you and the wife of your youth, with whom you have dealt treacherously; Yet she is your companion and your wife by covenant. But did He not make them one, having a remnant of the Spirit? And why one? He seeks godly offspring. Therefore take heed to your spirit, and let none deal treacherously with the wife of his youth. "For the Lord God of Israel says that He hates divorce, for it covers one's garment with violence," says the Lord of hosts. "Therefore take heed to your spirit that you do not deal treacherously. You have wearied the Lord with your words; Yet you say, in what way have we wearied Him?" In that you say, "Everyone who does evil is good in the sight of the Lord, and He delights in them, "Or, "Where is the God of justice?"

Terry Lursen

Matthew Henry's commentary on Malachi 2:10-17, best illuminates this scripture passage. I find it most difficult to add to his words:

Corrupt practices are the fruit of corrupt principles; he who is false to his God, will not be true to his fellow mortals. In contempt of the marriage covenant which God instituted, the Jews put away the wives they had of their own nation, probably to make room for strange wives. They made their lives bitter to them, yet, in the sight of others, they pretend to be tender of them. Consider she is thy wife, thy own; the nearest of the relation thou hast in the world. The wife is to be looked on, not as a servant, but as a companion to the husband. There is an oath of God between them which is not to be trifled with. Man and wife should continue to their live's end, in holy love and peace. Did not God make one, one Eve for one Adam. Yet God could have made another Eve.

Wherefore did He make but one woman for one man? It was that the children might be made a seed to serve Him. Husbands and wives must live in the fear of God, that their seed may be a godly seed. The God of Israel saith that He hateth putting away. Those who would be kept from sin, must take heed to their spirits, for there all sin begins.

Men will find that their wrong conduct in their families springs forth from selfishness, which disregards the welfare and happiness of others, when opposed to their own passions and fancies. It is wearisome to God to hear people to justify themselves in wicked practices. Those who think God can be a friend to sin, affront Him, and deceive themselves. The scoffers said, where is the God of judgment? But the day of the Lord will come.

The Unbecoming of America

Have you ever understood at all precisely what thinking is, what you experience when you think, anything at all? . . . You say to yourself: "I think that, when you have an opinion, when you form a judgment. In fact, to pass a judgment, true or false, is an act of thought; this act consists in feeling that there is a connection, a relation . . . , To think, as you see, is always to feel, and is nothing other than to feel. [1]

Thinking . . . forming opinions in the mind, based on relations, and that from one relation to another, is formed by those relations to itself. To the informed, the relations are built on first principles, foundational facts and truths that are eternal. To the uninformed, the relations are built on the lesser than. These are sayings built on ideological hearsay, and beliefs from another time, or from what is happening in the current, but not at all eternal. Do I dwell in conjecture, or do I dwell in one form of related unsubstantiated belief, but because it is related, therefore, it must be true. Does truth matter, when the definition of a thing lies undefined and is misconstrued as truth, when it is actually only an opinion? If you say, that my truth is my truth and your truth is your truth, and her truth is her truth; aren't you speaking of perspective, rather than first principle?

"So, as people say, it is impossible for anything to come into being unless there is something there beforehand." [2] The relation to thought built upon thought that came from another thought is the intricate building of a belief system about a thing, an ideology, for example. How is it that some people think in a particular way that seems to be rather exclusive, and yet many in the mainstream actually perpetuate the thought in their everyday life. Still others, think that what they see today is all there is, there is little thought given to what may be tomorrow and yesterday is a vapor, therefore there could not be any consequence for what I have done, or what I may do today. . . the pure form of non-relational sequencing particularly indigenous to the poverty mentality.

"What we are seeking are the principles and causes of the things that are..." [3]

If I find myself continually seeking for what makes this person think this way and this other person think in a totally contrasting way, is it possible to be objective in the course? For judgments are formed from thoughts that are formed from relations from other thoughts; are any objective, is it possible to abide in objectivity when the writer's belief abides in a first principle that there is a God and He knows all. Most of the greatest of philosophers and writers through the ages have believed that, and yet, ideologies most prevalent today scourge at the notion that there could possibly be a higher power than their own SELF or their system.

In conversations with perceived intellectuals, at times, as striking as it may seem, these intellectuals do not have a former or current knowledge at their disposal of their ideology, but they remain inexplicably consistent to their ideology all the while disregarding their uninformed dogmatism. Ideology, particularly in the reflexive domains of social liberalism, African socialism, and Christian fundamentalism, seemingly seek to protect themselves through the use of distraction,

The Dissolution of Truth

implied and un-implied ignorance, focused issues, and repressed hostility (i.e., just watch any ideologue when someone disagrees with him/her). These ideologies, among others, seek to take over whatever they are able to and protect their 'system' at all costs.

The progressive liberal, for example, has seen, either first hand, or from relation, the benefit of the social liberal system. This system 'takes care of me', or my family, or 'it takes care of the poor so that I don't have to', or, 'it takes care of the poor because that's what Jesus would have us do.' The Big Daddy, whether it is in the religious setting or in the government setting creates an undying, fervent dependency upon itself for itself and its own personal gain. This is the proverbial 'You will vote for me if I take care of you and yours...because I pretend that I care.'

I have seen the gamut from the ignorant to the most secure of intellectuals conform to the social liberalist ideology. The prevalent thought today is that an intellectual person will think like a liberal because they're smarter than 'those dumb conservatives who believe in God'. The commonality of progressive thought is sown in such a way as to persuade all that their way is the higher, nobler way. And, that the rest of the populace will one day progress and mature to where they are. It is as though the system itself is a spirit guiding the believers into a version of 'truth' that has always been and is where America should be headed. To the social liberalist, anyone who does not adhere to their belief is backward, uneducated, and needs to be guided into the 'faith' of their belief system. Domains of reflexivity such as this are dangerous. If you could ask Bonhoeffer, he would tell you so. Interestingly, though, it sounds like I'm talking about Christian fundamentalism...doesn't it?

Terry Lursen

There has to be a supreme basis of foundation from first principles in order for demonstrative knowledge to arrive at a proper conclusion. (Aristotle). If the ideology cannot provide substantive proof from demonstrated knowledge that the ideology, in reality, truly works, then whatever conclusions that are derived from the ideology necessarily need to be dismissed. If the ideology cannot be sustained in regression back to first principles, then, where did the idea come from?

For example, where did the idea of imperialistic microcredit come from? Indonesia? Do you see what foreign ideology has done to our banking industry?

It is, perhaps, the irrational state of the social liberalist to contend in self-protection modes of debate because the ideology is not formed from first principles, but is indeed formed from the thoughts of men, long ago, needing power, rather than the need of the populace to be taken care of. Ideologies lacking first principle thought lack foundational belief and rely upon the misapplication of facts to support their hypotheses, manipulate thought and opinion through misinformation, construe innuendo to defame their opponents, threaten the disloyal, and prove daily that they really do not know what they are doing. These people may, or may not be intellectual. The spirit of the system is an equal opportunity destroyer.

The self-aggrandizement of the leaders of the propagating philosophy has become perpetual to the wishful demise of any corporation making a sincere profit. Profits grow companies and the current ideology of social liberalism desires that businesses act un-becoming themselves for the betterment of the entire population. I suppose that the government would then be the FATHER of the populace to

The Dissolution of Truth

disperse the profits to the poor, but then you would have the presidents and the politicians giving away that which they did not work for and it would all be gone soon.

Terry Lursen

On Personal Relationships

It was in ancient Greece that Epictetus perceived that, "We are disturbed not by events, but by the views we take of them." [1]

Doing the right thing the wrong way gets the thing accomplished, but leaves an indelible, negative, lasting impression that is not soon forgotten.

The perceived immaturity of another person beckons for the same. If I respond to another's immaturity (i.e., their out of order behavior) with immaturity, I then cease to be God in the earth in the moment. The situation then becomes rather worldly, flesh eating flesh, as opposed to iron sharpening iron. It is the Christ in me, the hope of glory that the other person so desperately needs, as I do myself. It is His glory that should rise within me, rather than some vain response of self-protection, or a worse self-aggrandizement of believing that I know and am willing to express something that I actually do not.

Pride and arrogance believe that they can displace true authority. I have to be completely denied for the true authority to be revealed in a time of response to a less than holy situation. It is no longer I, then, but the Christ living in me that brings reality to fruition. The other person should have the opportunity to be responded to by the Holy Spirit, Himself, even as the archangel Michael, "...in contending

The Dissolution of Truth

with the devil, when he disputed about the body of Moses, dared not bring against him a reviling accusation, but said, 'The Lord rebuke you!'" (Jude 9) We often tread where angels dare not.

Oftentimes a response should not be rendered as to give way to a lower road. It is again, through the denial of self that our Lord Jesus taught us,

He was oppressed and He was afflicted, Yet He opened not His mouth; He was led as a lamb to the slaughter, And as a sheep before its shearers is silent, So He opened not His mouth. (Isaiah 53:7)

This leads us to an errant religious teaching that you simply let people run over you because you think you're acting like Jesus. This is not scriptural. Jesus knew who He was and He walked in that authority. He knew what He had to do and that was to suffer and die on a cross. He did so in obedience. By not opening His mouth, He was essentially saying that He did not worry, complain, murmur, or speak ill of His Father for His Divine purpose. His destiny was to be the atonement for our sin by dying on a cross. That was HIS purpose. Our purpose in Him is wrapped in the swaddling clothes of desiring Him, denying the Self, taking up our cross, and following Him. His purpose was specific and NO ONE else could have, nor could ever perform His particular purpose, it's already done. God had to do it Himself.

If my cross takes me to a place of circumstance wherein my circumstances require me to respond to darkness, I find that I cannot respond on a human level in a godly manner. I can't, but He can. He has proven that. And I have proven that I am humanly incapable of responding from the heavenlies as God, but He can and does. He does the responding through me. I've seen it. I've experienced Him responding to darkness through me in some extremely grave situations.

What a dreadful soul I am if all I have is me to respond to the dark forces in varying opportunities of distress and baited temptation. However, it is the abandonment to the Spirit of God that beckons me to Him, His love will not let me go, nor will it allow me to continue in myself as myself. I am abandoned to Him. It is this denial and the presenting of the true self as a living sacrifice that He makes holy... that He makes righteous...that He lives and moves and breathes and in Him I find Life.

"For whoever desires to save his life will lose it, but whoever loses his life for My sake will find it." (Matthew 16:25)

This life that we are to find is the life of who we were before the beginning:

For You formed my inward parts;

You covered me in my mother's womb.

I will praise you, for I am fearfully and wonderfully made;

Marvelous are Your works,

And that my soul knows very well.

My frame was not hidden from You,

When I was made in secret,

And skillfully wrought in the lowest parts of the earth.

Your eyes saw my substance, being yet unformed.

And in Your book they all were written,

The days fashioned for me, When as yet there were none of them. (Psalm 139:13-16)

The Dissolution of Truth

If we will always be, then we have always been, but we will not always be as we have always been.

What I am after by continually submitting to Him is for the Divine Nature to be revealed. Paul said, "Therefore since we are the offspring of God, we ought not to think that the Divine Nature is like gold or silver or stone, something shaped by art or man's devising." (Acts 17:29)

You cannot shape God into a cross, or put Him in a box. You cannot act like, or be like Jesus. The Divine Nature is absolute. There is only one God and He must be Himself in me. If I try to act like Him, I fail. I attempt the temptation of usurpation. I am not He. He Is. He Is One. The best that I could be is a miserable substitute; that's what religion is...a miserable substitute.

Religion sets itself up to be an idol unto itself with its own laws and traditions. Religion is a false substitute for the Divine Nature. And if I continue to believe that 'I' can do the work, then my pride will steal the very best that God has for me through my own willful persuasion into an abyss of what does not matter.

I cannot transform myself into the Divine Nature, but I can transform myself into the work of transgressing. (2 Corinthians 11:10-15)

I have to go through the Door of the Kingdom of God and stay there. There is hidden treasure there, but it is His hidden treasure that has to be shared with the people I come in contact with. That is how I am to respond in my circumstance, no matter what circumstance that presents itself to me in any given moment. I am in all things tried.

The institutional church, too, is in all things tried and has fallen short from the Truth. It is, perhaps, why the description of a 'hate' crime has been created as it has today because, over a period of many years, the world's view of the church's love is that of hate from the church's response being so despicable towards other humans.

Will I follow the legions of men who have gone before me and proclaimed the cross of Christ through a vessel of hate, or will I be True to the Truth that I know to be True in me?

The Dynamics of Spiritual Truth

While on a recent trip, I was out one morning and another gentleman insisted that I look up to the sky, specifically into the sun. Immediately, I thought it to be a strange demand coming from someone that I did not know, but his inquisitive smile and pleasant demeanor enabled me to concede to his polite demand.

As I looked up straight into the late morning sun, I was able to see what he saw. It was something that neither one of us had ever seen. He, being much older than myself, marveled at the sight. I gladly marveled with him.

I am certain that it was something that science could easily explain, still I cannot, but all could see who chose to. There, surrounding the bright morning sun was a perfect rainbow in a perfect circle completely surrounding the sun. I have seen many a rainbow in my time, and the sight of such does bring a sense of joy and awareness of the atmosphere around us with the mixture of light and water vapor. The elements of sunshine and rainfall are typically required for a rainbow, and the sight of the rainbow is typically away from the sun.

It had not rained, not in our locale, that is, and we were looking straight at the sun around 11 am that morning. The circle of rainbow around the sun dynamically was perfect. Although science could explain it, I believe that only God could create such a sight to behold. It was indeed majestic.

I speak about this event, not to conjure up some deep spiritual meaning to life, but to bring us to some type of realization, an acknowledge of sorts, that not everyone saw what we saw that day. It was not in the television news, that I'm aware of; nor was it found as an explosive phenomenon on the internet news either. It was what it was and whoever saw it saw it in its glory, and after an hour, it was gone. I still see it in my mind, as clear as it was in those moments.

What I do want us to see are facts, facts as we see facts, rather than illusions that others tell us what we see or don't see.

If that man had told me that he saw a rainbow around the sun that morning, and I, having not seen it, probably would have looked at him with a strange look of non-verbal retort and lifted eyebrow, stating, 'Why are you telling me this?' Or, 'Are you sure you saw what you saw?' Or, 'That's a little unusual, and the not so common thing to see, I've never seen that before...' and then go on my way with very little concern for his sighting of something that was so majestic. It was indescribably breathtaking.

It was a scientific fact that we saw what we saw and can most probably be fully and easily explained by a meteorologist, or high school science teacher. It was there and no one can tell me that it wasn't.

As science facts are facts, as gravity is as real as throwing a ball up into the air and expecting the law of gravity to exert itself onto the ball to bring it back to my hand...so are Biblical, spiritual facts just as real and existent as science facts. The scientist may say that his facts

The Dissolution of Truth

are clearly and undeniably provable and mine are not since one cannot 'prove' God.

However, Biblical facts are based on faith. If you have the God kind of faith to believe that God is, that the Bible is the Word of God, then you believe that in faith. If you do not believe that God is, or that the Bible is the Word of God, then you simply do not believe that; I, nor anyone else can make that a fact for you, you simply do not believe. I have no argument with you, your argument is with God.

My current personal belief, contrary to contemporary beliefs of apologetics, faith cannot be argued. The scriptures cannot be, nor do they need to be, defended to an unbeliever. If the unbeliever does not believe in God, does not have faith, does not believe that the Word of God is what it is, no human being is going to convince that unbeliever of those 'faith facts' because the first requirement to believing the faith facts is faith. [1] If you do not believe those foundational facts about God, Jesus, and the Word of God, you simply do not have the faith to believe. Because one does not have the faith to believe, does not mean that they do not exist, for they do, you simply do not believe it.

One may contend here based on their non-existent empirical knowledge that God does not exist, but any supposed empirical knowledge would be skewed because one would have to believe the knowledge derived based on the belief that their knowledge is forthwith, undeniable and proven through experience and no such knowledge exists. Or, does it? Is there undeniable knowledge existing in our natural realm that proves the non-existence of God...in someone's mind, someone has the ability to not believe, but only in their mind.

Terry Lursen

God is Spirit and those who worship Him, worship Him in spirit and in truth. There is no other way to worship God, other than the way that He has said it in His Word. For someone to not adhere to the Word of God because they do not believe, is entirely believable and has been since its creation. However, even non-belief is a belief in the non-belief order of things and sets the human on a course that is foretold in the Word of God.

Because it requires faith to believe faith facts, it would also require faith to believe in the absolute certainty of absolute truth. Everyone has an opinion, or a perspective, just as they have an armpit, or two. Value justification is as such. But, here, we are not talking about perspective, opinion, value, appraisal, or perception. Here, we seek after truth, and the truth that I know to be true is the Truth of God. He is certain. He is undeniable and unchanging. Jesus said that He is the Truth and the Life, I believe that to be true. And, it is True, whether you or I believe it, or not.

For a man to say that he is a Christian is to say that he believes that Jesus is Lord, that the Word of God is True, and that man would also be saying that he walks in the Light as He is in the Light. These are all faith facts within the Word itself. Confession of Jesus Christ is not just an audible verbal opening of the mouth saying, 'I believe', oh no, it is far more than that. Confession means that every particle of my being not only believes, but lives in, abides in, that Truth, and so walks according to that belief system that is so very well descriptive in the scriptures.

A man who calls himself Christian is man who lives and abides in the Word, Jesus, out of love for His Father Who brought him into the Light. Obedience is wrought from love, the same love that He gave us.

The Dissolution of Truth

A Christian does not pick and choose his verses of obedience, for that is neither obedience, nor love, nor truthful.

A man is not a Christian just because he says he grew up in a Christian household. The mere expression of that belief is an ignorant acknowledgement that he is unaware of what the Word of God says as well as expressing ignorance of the abiding relationship that ensues in the walk of a Christian walking in the Light of grace. If a man will, out of ignorance, or knowledge, lie about the allegiance that he is supposed to walk in, his life is a life of an actor, a hypocrite, who is incapable of knowing truth and walking in it.

Spiritual truths are believed by spiritual men who are led by the Spirit of God. These spiritual truths are spiritual facts believed in faith. Unbelief in the non-existence of these truths is unbelief indeed and that person is just as real as any spiritual man that ever walked the earth.

The person who does not believe has conscripted himself to the ranks of the unbelief and has wagered the bet that Pascal warned us of so many years ago, "If God does not exist, one will lose nothing by believing in Him, while if He does exist, one will lose everything by not believing." [2]

Apparent Contradictions

Have you ever been lied to by someone you trust, and you didn't know that you were being lied to?

Public prayer, especially our corporate prayers, are oftentimes, imitations from past religious observances, but do not have to be.

God loves the aroma of a good bar-b-q. It certainly is not the smell of unclean flesh.

To talk about isolated spiritual experiences reveals that is all you have in your spiritual walk and you may or may not even be on the pathway of God.

On imitation: We have been preached at to 'Be like Jesus', or 'What would Jesus Do?', or 'A Christian would not act that way'. Have you ever known anyone that acted like Jesus Christ?

Recently, in a house of worship, the young guest preacher told the congregation, as he was preparing to teach on the Beatitudes in Matthew 5, that the world looks at the church and if the church doesn't live up to Jesus' commands there, the world has the right to judge the church for not living up to the Word. Although this does occur, it is a lie. No unbeliever has the 'right' to judge the church save God Himself and the church, itself. The church, for centuries, has been told to 'be good', to do what Jesus says, and the world certainly does look at the church in judgment knowing that the church has not lived up to

The Dissolution of Truth

its own expectations. Outsiders look at the failures of the church and call it antiquated, dogmatic, unloving, and hateful. If someone inside the church talks about the Truth of the Gospel to the outside world, it is received with bitterness and derogatory thought. The church has perpetuated the self-inflicted judgment from the world because of its apparent lack of the knowledge of the Word of God.

"But he who is spiritual judges all things, yet he himself is rightly judged by no one." (1 Corinthians 2:15)

"I wrote to you in my epistle not to keep company with sexually immoral people. Yet i certainly did not mean with the sexually immoral people of this world, or with the covetous, or extortioners, or idolaters, since then you would need to go out of the world. But now I have written to you not to keep company with anyone named a brother, who is sexually immoral, or covetous, or an idolater, or a reviler, or a drunkard, or an extortioner - not even to eat with such a person. For what do I have to do with judging those who are outside? Do you not judge those who are on the inside? But those who are on the outside, God judges. Therefore 'put away from yourselves the evil person.'" (1 Corinthians 5:9-13)

Has this critical thought regarding the fellowship of believers justified, or is it just the world looking back at the church as unrepentant?

For centuries, most of the leaders of the church have either knowingly or unknowingly lied to their followers for so many reasons; they cannot all be listed here. The main reasons would be lack of knowledge of the Word, forced traditions, buildings and architecture, power, self-aggrandizement, fame, duplicitous teachings, money, money, and more money.

Terry Lursen

The foremost problem with the institutional church believing the lie that the world has the right to judge them is that it is impossible, first of all, to BE LIKE JESUS, because only Jesus Christ could be Jesus Christ, and you, if you are called by His name could never live up to what He was. He was God in the flesh.

If you are called by His name to name the name of Christ for yourself, it is He Who does the saving, and it is He Who has done the work. It is He Who keeps you saved from your sin, and it is all about Him, not you.

Secondly, God will judge the world. That is one less concern that, as a Christian, that you would need to put onto your person. The world has no right to defame you, judge you, ridicule you, or persecute you. They will do those things, but they have no inherent right to, it is the devil's lie.

If you call yourself Christian, stand up, with a backbone and deny yourself before Him, not the world...and in His Holy love; love in Spirit and in Truth.

The Dissolution of Truth

Believing Unbelief

Can you convince an unbeliever, one who forthrightly chooses not to believe, the Truth? Can you, if they have chosen their way, the road of unbelief?

Can you make someone believe something that they deliberately choose not to believe, with fervor and extreme prejudice, they believe their beliefs. Their unbelief is so strong it is as an impenetrable fortress surrounding their mind in deep layers of hewn stone. Their legions of thought and beliefs protect their fortress to disallow any Light of Truth to dispel any darkness prevailing within their fortified walls of unbelief.

They see what they see how they see it from how they have been taught by the spirit of the ages through the worthless shepherds of old. Propagators of beliefs from the ancients to receive unto themselves the blessings of the peoples they control. Is there anything new under the sun?

Liars giving pretense of the womb of care when only availing the misguided a way of escape into a burning pit of despair. The ancient takes his shovel and heaves the fatherless into the pit of the unborn where there dwells an unquenchable fire. He smiles a smile in his continued work of destruction and death of agony and pain.

It is to the pitied and the poor that the liar lies his lies to make way for the more...to cover them in wrappings of sewn cloth, glistening white, yet in bondage they be to their belief as to their dismay that they chose to believe the unbeliever as their way of escape.

For it is the way of escape all look to see from the demise on this earth of clay and leaf. The way of the many and the way of the few; it is to him who believes.

It is what we choose to believe is what we will choose to serve. It is in service that we are known on this earth, but it is in what we choose to believe that we are known in the heavens.

Is Truth, the Truth of the absolute, or is it what you choose to believe? Does a man know his way, can he know it? It is for certain that we are born, and it is for certain we will die. It is in the day of the Lord that men choose the in-between. There is neither luck, nor chance in your circumstance.

Men see what they see by what they have seen and it is what they have seen that keeps them where they are. What do you see, son of man, what do you see? The power of the Holy Spirit that gives men hope, that gives men sight, that is Who I see.

On Being Nefarious

To be nefarious is to be flagrantly wicked, evil, to perform wicked acts, impious...to be irreverent, lacking in respect of God, or your parents. [1]

It is to seduce is to persuade to disobedience or disloyalty.

Sedition - incitement of resistance to or insurrection against lawful authority. [2] (ibid.)

Is anyone exempt before a Holy God?

I am not. Our human nature to satisfy our own will makes us culpable to almost anything if given the perfect opportunity, which is just another reason for us to refrain from judging others when they fall.

Holiness - Set aside, sacred, perfection, spiritually pure. [3] (ibid.)

Is there a definition for holiness that is real and true? Can we even begin to fathom holiness?

Most likely, the majority of us do not consider ourselves nefarious. Terrorists, murdering mobsters, punishers, slave traders, and the like would be considered part of the group, along with a host of others of hideous distinction.

But when it comes to holiness, would my thoughts and words be those reflecting murder, sedition, or any other sort of wickedness otherwise known as nefarious?

When we compare ourselves with ourselves, we tend to overlook our tendencies so as not to be too hard on ourselves, besides, 'I'm not stealing, not murdering, not participating in sex slave trafficking, etc., not in the flesh anyway.'

When Jesus said, "You have heard that it was said to those of old, 'You shall not murder, and whoever murders will be in danger of the judgment.' But I say to you that whoever is angry with his brother without a cause shall be in danger of the judgment. And whoever says to his brother, 'Raca!' shall be in danger of the council. But whoever says, 'You fool!' shall be in danger of hellfire...You have heard that it was said to those of old, 'You shall not commit adultery.' But I say to you that whoever looks at a woman to lust for her has already committed adultery with her in his heart." (Matthew 5:21-22, 27-28)

It is what is in our hearts that will determine our pleasure to please our anger, our eyes, or our even our ears in justification of sedition. The word of someone who is supposed to be telling us the truth, but is not, is just as wicked as any other sin.

Words written on a page, or spoken in the air, should be the truth, without exception.

If you, as the reader take exception to this writing because you believe something about yourself that in no way do you have any guilt of relationship to wickedness, then I would have to commend you for your holiness.

The word of God in Romans 8:1 says, "There is therefore no condemnation to those who are 'in' (parentheses mine) Christ Jesus,

The Dissolution of Truth

who do not walk according to the flesh, but according to the Spirit."

But since I am still in this world, and as Jesus would say, 'not of it', I still find myself asking myself, 'What have you done? What did you say? What are you thinking? What are you looking at?' In my own self-examination, I find my own acts of lust and idolatry, of envy and hate. Most times, I correct myself, without condemning myself, for I know that I am 'in' Him.

When His Spirit corrects me, then all my words fall back to the examiners table to discover their origin and their placement. I have submitted to Him to be examined by Him at any time for it is He Who keeps me in Him, and while I am in the holy place, nothing that is not holy is allowed. It is His righteousness and not my own, I know, but I know that I can do better in my thinking, better in my communicating, and better at listening to Him, the source of Truth. There truly is no condemnation to those who are in Christ Jesus, walking in the light as He is in the light, and in that, I find comfort. His thoughts and ways are higher than ours. It is His holiness that separates and sets Him far above what we would call good.

He is building me in Him to be truth in the earth as it is with all those who call themselves Christian. Because of my will, being true to Him first is not automatic, and I see that now. Being true to Him always I will to be some day.

Terry Lursen

Peace – The Treasure That You Seek

There are not many people on this earth who do not desire peace and happiness in some way. It is a reality that most of the people I have known in my lifetime, including myself, have desired and searched for peace in their lives, their marriages, their work, their homes, and most particularly, their inner being. Peace, it seems, is elusive to the many, costly for some, and non-existent for others. Peace is what most people are searching for when they are saying they are searching for God. For most folk, if they are able to realize a few moments of perceived peace, they will forgo any further spiritual journey immediately following their momentary lapse of stress and turmoil. For the many, it is too easy to get up and walk away from God.

It is most extraordinary for us humans in that we have been led to believe that we can presumably search for God, in Jesus name, and at the drop of that name, peace can show up in our inner most being. Is it really that easy? Whether it is that easy, or not, is not the main issue here, for the presumption is that what the human is doing is seeking peace, rather than seeking the God Who is peace.

The Word of God most emphatically says to "pursue peace with all people…" (Hebrews 12:14), "seek peace and pursue it…" (Psalm 34:14), and in 1 Peter 3:11, "seek peace and pursue it…."

The Dissolution of Truth

This is where most Christians find themselves, and those who espouse themselves to be Christian, in the place of seeking the benefit of the Presence of God without truly seeking the benefactor Himself. Even the mere fact of me taking these few verses out of their context is how most people live their lives, out of context with Truth, and out of context with reality. The American Christian is profoundly culpable here in that we have been taught by our teachers and preachers that we can purchase some value from God for a gift to a ministry, or purchase a gift from God for rightly serving Him, or the said ministry. These cases range from the misunderstanding of to the misuse of to the abuse of God's Word and His Holy Presence.

His Holy peace is found in Him, in His Presence.

Hebrews 12:4, "Pursue peace with all people, and holiness, without which no one will see the Lord."

Psalm 34:13-14, "Keep your tongue from evil, and your lips from speaking deceit. Depart from evil and do good; seek peace and pursue it."

1 Peter 3:10-12 is a direct quote reference to Psalm 34:13-14, and adds, "For the eyes of the Lord are on the righteous, and His ears are open to their prayers; but the face of the Lord is against those who do evil."

Ezekiel 7:25, "Destruction comes; They will seek peace, but there shall be none..."

Ephesians 2:14, "For He Himself is our peace, who has made both one, and has broken down the middle wall of separation..."

Terry Lursen

John 14:27, "Peace I leave with you, My peace I give to you; not as the world gives do I give to you. Let not your heart be troubled, neither let it be afraid."

The context of seeking peace from the Lord is always within the context of being with, or in Him. He is our peace. Christ, who is our peace, is the Truth. For those who are seeking heaven, they are seeking peace, peace from their existence, peace from their everyday life, peace from their torment, peace in their finances, their families, their being and peace in their future.

Dietrich Bonhoeffer stated that what people needed was not peace, but Jesus. [1]

For those who have chosen to command the peace of God from God, as though they could draw a morsel from His Presence, is likened to drawing His blood from His veins and have it run into their veins to settle them down in peace, like a drug...with the motive to using the God of peace for their own personal preference of immediate need, only to discard Him when they are rested.

When Jesus commanded the waves, and said, 'Peace, be still', He was talking to the waves, not commanding His Father. (Mark 4:39) It is a disrespectful abuse to command, or order our heavenly Father to our beckon call. It is a complete misrepresentation of the Word of God to use the Word of God against Him to satisfy our earthly pleasures and desires.

It is only in the mind of man that he believes that he can use God for his personal preferences to call on Him in times of trouble and then wickedly discard Him and walk away from an omnipresent Presence. That is the power of the foolishness of man. The mind of man in his selfish desire to please himself in peace and then relieve himself on His Creator...it is only in his mind he has done this thing and shown his true motive and worth to an Almighty God.

The motives of the mind of man are tried and are faithless. The thoughts of mankind are not the thoughts of a Holy God. It is for a time that man dwells on the earth and for a season of time he persists. Let those who are called according to His Name, be found faithful, unwavering in the belief that He Is, abiding in Him as He Is, being found true to Him as He Is and no longer walking in a way that only seeks a morsel when, in reality, He seeks all that we are, and when He gets that, we get into all of Him.

I pray that we become that which we seek in Him, true peace, as Christ, Who is our peace, living in us. There is peace through His Presence in Him, in His Kingdom, the dwelling place of God.

"Blessed are the poor in spirit, for theirs is the kingdom of heaven." (Matthew 5:3)

Terry Lursen

Heighten the Sight

Oftentimes, many of us find ourselves in squeamish territories brought on by our external circumstances, or by self-imposed skirmishes of the mind. Most of our trials are of the latter kind. I have found it to be quite interesting how many folk will dwell in anxiety for prolonged periods of time and if, by chance, one tries to bring them out of it, resentment seems to be the order of the day.

Are we to try and take these things from our fellow humans, or are we to allow them to wallow in self-pity until the season of self-pity has passed? Trying to take that which is not yours to take brings with it a burden not too wholesome a life worthwhile.

It is of grave maturity to see that the circumstances and things of our fellows are there for a reason and although they may be placed by human hands, they are engineered by that which is not, and they are not looking to be removed by human hands. What is it that we see that our fellow cannot see that he sees what he sees and is unable to see from the height of the sight of a higher horizon? It is not of presumption that there is a higher sight view, it is one of belief that pride will not allow ourselves to see what others see about ourselves or our situation.

We do not see all things, for we see what we see from our level of sight at the viewpoint of the level. We all are in our circumstances

The Dissolution of Truth

and none are exempt from the cares of the day. Decisions born from clarity are brought about because they have been viewed from different perspectives, but many of us are capricious when we make decisions and suffer the ensuing consequences as a result.

The desire and the ability to heighten the sight of us all in order to rise from our circumstances is so vitally necessary that it behooves us to gain insight as to how do we achieve a higher sight plain when viewing our prevailing circumstances. We would all agree that we see more from the mountain top than from the valley below. Wisdom, knowledge, and experience are on the mountain top, as well as, spiritual insight known only to the ones who are willing to submit to the Spirit who gives the insight.

We need each other. I need my fellow man because, in my humanity, I either refuse to go to the mountain top, or forget to, in the midst of my circumstance. The conundrum in the whirlwind of our minds keeps us preoccupied with unending distractions. Unsolved problems cause consternation and we are unrelenting in our abiding in our self-pity rather than seeking Truth from a higher plain. Heighten your sight. Rise above your circumstance and you will see things yet unseen. Heighten the horizon and you will be able to see what is coming rather than being buried by it. Oswald Chambers continues to teach me that it is not so much my responsibility to alter things as it is to remain true to God in the midst of it. (The Complete Works of Oswald Chambers, page 662-669)

The ability to make a great decision is waning in our nation today. I see what I see from the vantage point of my peers. Who have you surrounded yourself with? Where do you dwell? Where is your mind? Who are you listening to? If it's no one, you are in trouble indeed. If it's everyone, the worse still. If it's entertainment, you will dwell in a tiny facade of unreality that leads to a path in a crevice of an earthquake yet to come.

Who are you listening to? Do you know the difference between the mountain top and the valley? Have you paid the price of the distance between the two?

In the Kingdom of God, there is the opportunity to be seated in heavenly places. (Ephesians 2:6-7) The price of admission has been paid, but you have to leave your Self at the door.

The sight from the height of the heavenly places is real and true. What do you see from your where you sit?

And from the height of the heavenly places...what do you see, son of man, what do you see?

The Great Illusion

A few things that I have seen under the sun and a few things I have learned and one is this: it is far easier for a man to work with his hands than it is to work with his mind.

I have done both. I have worked with my mind and I have worked with my hands.

With my hands, I have torn down, built up, torn down again, reworked, cut, cut out and cut down; I have made and unmade, dug and filled, cleaned, scrubbed, and sterilized; with my hands I have picked up and thrown down, I have tossed and caught, turned and flipped...all with my hands. With my hands I have broken, sliced, and diced, cooked and seared, grilled and washed, and washed again. I have washed my hands a few times. With my hands I have bathed and showered, touched and remade. With my hands I have taken, given, wrapped, unwrapped, written and erased. I have given and taken, moved and created, with my hands, I have loved and I have hated... all with my hands. I have embraced and I have rejected; I have said hello and I have said good-bye.

With my mind, I have created, toiled, and stressed. I have written, read, added, and multiplied, subtracted and divided, all with my mind. With my mind, I have embraced, loved and despised, rejected, and received rejection. With my mind, I have worked, thought, and thought some more. I have analyzed, rationalized, reasoned, and grown. I have learned, learned, and learned. With my mind I see and hear, I grope and walk. I see the light with my mind; I dream dreams and see visions. With my mind, I understand and am enlightened and with my mind I am played the fool and have walked in folly.

In my mind, I have feared and lost; I have won and succeeded. In my mind, I move to higher ground and sit in heavenly places. With my mind, I think and it is with my mind I receive the thoughts of a king with its intention for another time.

With my mind, I see beyond, I see what is. It is with my mind I see truth and understand. Yes, it is far easier to work with one's hands than it is to work with one's mind. For what is it in the mind of man that he can create and bring to fruition with only his mind? How can a man succeed and advance with only his mind?

For it is in the mind of man to work with his hands, after all, it is his purpose, isn't it? Or, is it? Is it man's purpose to work with his hands, or is it his purpose to see what was and bring to fruition what is?

I have seen men rewarded greatly for both, but to work with one's mind, the reward is higher, nobler, and more rewarding, isn't it? I have seen the rewards of the hands rewarded greatly these days.

So, is it easier for a man to work with his hands than it is to work with his mind? I say, yes, and for this reason, but not this reason alone. It is easier to work with one's hands than it is to work with one's mind because it is what man sees upon the work until its completion that a man will work with his hands. It is the immediate response of a thing done, accomplished. It is what he sees that enjoins him to see what he sees. It is the material. It is what he eats, touches, lays his eyes

The Dissolution of Truth

upon, and turns his attention to that is the material. It is a thing rather than a thought. It is something gold, green, or blue, but it is a thing that will never last that men hope for most and it is that thing, that whatever thing, that men will work for with their hands to obtain, only to lose it and attempt to obtain it again.

It is with a man's hands that he eats, for if he does not work, he should not eat. To the work a man goes with his mind or his hands or with his hands and his mind. I would choose the latter. For I have done both, worked with my hands and worked with my hands and my mind. Enjoin the mind. Mind the mind and you will mind your work.

It is to the thinking man that he is not sold by the salesman, the proprietor of ideas, he is as he thinks he is, but is not. For his is the work of the illusionist, who works a work with the work of his hands, but what is being worked is his mind and not yours. Work with your mind. Know what is real and true.

It is with your mind that you believe or choose not to believe. It is with your mind that you choose to forgive, love, and embrace. It is with your mind, you choose to know truth and truth that remains is all that will remain.

You see, it is far easier to work with one's hands than it is to work with one's mind, even though it is a far better thought to have thought about what is, and what is to come, than it is not to think and to work another day and believe that that is all there is.

It is a far easier thing to do to kill, steal, and destroy, than it is to create. The work that a man chooses to do will reveal his life in his beliefs as his beliefs reveal the work of his hands and the work of his mind.

It is also a far easier thing to bounce, kick, hit, or throw a ball. There are grown men playing children's games for hire. The indulgence of entertainment of the populace has always been with us. This is most definitely not the observance of the amateur Olympian who has played his game and worked his work to become the best in the world for a season. I salute the Olympian.

But it is in our day, the indulgence of the professional ball player that continues beyond the appearance of reality into the most definitive working of the hands into a land of illusion. It is to these professional men, these hirelings, that their illusion is their reality and they exchange the ability to bounce, kick, hit, or throw a ball, of all things, into dollars of such great magnitude that the children of the day can only dream dreams to be like them...to be able to play children's games for the rest of their lives and never quite grow up. Immature children getting paid great sums of money offers the illusion of greatness. In all of life, there is nothing great about being able to bounce, throw, hit, or kick a ball, nothing great at all. But it is to the entertainer to entertain men's minds so that they do not have to think about what is or is to come. Entertainers playing to the entertained while the world watches and the beast slides in unaware.

Who will reckon the day of reckoning that the entertainer has had his last say? To the actor, the ultimate hypocrite, who plays the world as his stage and uses the minds of others as a tool for their gain. They wield their thoughts as a swordsman wields his sword because man chose to work with his hands thereby becoming a slave to the entertainer's demands. Who is next to be entertained? Who is next to be sold? The politician who chooses to use the entertainer as his tool

The Dissolution of Truth

chooses to be chosen in the great illusion for he knows neither life, nor truth, but only the illusion of the material, the next thing...the thing to be bartered. For the next thing to be bartered is our country, while men watch the entertainers entertain, not truly knowing what is and is to come.

What do you see, son of man?

Terry Lursen

The Opportunity of a Seed

A man's thoughts are not his own. The source of thoughts is far greater than the human heart. A man's thoughts are indigenous to him and are inculcated within his heart, but the source of the thought is a far different thing, especially in this overly egregious society of marketers and advertisers in America who constantly batter people with thoughts of a better product or service, or a better presidency.

The thought of a certain thought is mulled in the human mind, but that meditated thought, did it originate in that mind, or did it come from another source? I receive thoughts from the spirit realm, both the Holy Spirit and the lesser than. I receive thoughts and information through reading, revelation from the Holy Spirit in the reading of God's word, listening to the radio, music, words, other humans, letters, printed material, audio devices, nature, meditation, and on and on. I think what I think, but I am not so prideful as to think that my thoughts are original, they come from somewhere, and I will ruminate on a thought, whether it be good for me, or bad for me.

I have been sold and manipulated with thoughts and I have done the same to other people. I have been presented ideas through a speaker or a writer and I have listened and obtained, or I have rejected the ideas, but I have listened nonetheless.

It is to the salesman, the lawyer... turned politician who delves

The Dissolution of Truth

best into the world of transmitting thoughts into others that become as propaganda to the listening ear that is one of the most dangerous and manipulative of all communications. The reflexive society of the progressive has to propagandize upon the populace in order to replicate itself through the manipulation of the mind with a few choice words that translate into fear and the gathering together under the guise of protection from the onslaught of the supposed adversary who is trying to suffocate those in its path. The listener then becomes a victim and the propagandist becomes the savior to save the victim from the adversary. Fear, divisiveness, and untruths are the weapons of their warfare. Planting seed thoughts into the mind of the listener, no matter how untrue, will lodge into the crevice of the listener's mind to wait for another of raining down of the fertilizer of the more egregious manipulation called information.

The natural cause of reproduction does not have to manipulate to reproduce as our Lord has caused nature to do so with overwhelming positive effects. It is to man that the Lord said, "Then God said, 'Let us make man in Our image, according to Our likeness; let them have dominion...' (Genesis 1:26ff) It is over all things in the animal and plant kingdom on the earth that Man has dominion. It was and still is a gift from God. It is the order of things. The marriage bed was, and is, the way God intended for a man and his female wife to reproduce and to have continued dominion over the things of the earth.

But, when a man has to lie, cheat, and steal to influence presumed dominance over another man, or his children, it is to that liar, the progressive liberal, that he presumes his own failure upon himself. Ultimately, he is attempting to usurp our Lord as master over his populace in order to achieve a certain dominance that he chooses to take rather than allowing our Lord to be in authority; he takes the authority for himself ever how he can take it because it is not the means, but the end that is most important to the social liberal.

The implanting a seed thought is an opportunity of the propagandist to further his perceived advancement. This brings us to the supposed gaffe of our Vice-President Biden when he told a group in Danville, Virgina, "He said in his first 100 days, he's gonna let the big banks once again write their own rules. They're gonna put y'all back in chains." The crowd that he was speaking to was, for the most part, half white and half black. It is a southern city and he digressed to a southern accent when speaking those words. The context of the phrasing was banking and how Governor Romney's plan regarding banking in the future was, in the speaker's mind, being interpreted.

The context was banking, a white man's plan for banking. How is it, then that it becomes a white man's plan, when the speaker himself is white speaking to a racially mixed crowd, what would be the purpose in that?

There isn't much that is an accident, a 'gaffe', as the media likes to present information to its own populace. No, this was not a gaffe, this was something far more sinister and disturbing than Vice-President Biden's own protruding silliness would allow him to make. All things have a purpose, as do most, if not all words. We really do not know the purpose of all things and words as they occur, but when, in time, trends reveal their meanings and their meanings are not difficult to figure out to a thinking man who understands the laws of manipulation and cult propaganda.

The statements that the Vice President made are the result of his

The Dissolution of Truth

being with President Obama and are most likely how they talk when in private. This then released him to say it publicly. After all, Vice President Biden is a puppet of the Obama administration and the President enjoys the entertainment that Biden provides because, in the midst of the entertainment of VP Biden's presumed stupidity, which is not, for he is a puppet of the current regime; a seed thought of racism is planted in the minds of black people. Blacks across the nation were able to hear a white man, in a southern city, with a southern accent, say, "They're gonna put y'all back in chains." This is to say, "I'm one of ya'll and I'm warning ya'll 'bout 'dem white folk."

They know what they are doing, and even though conservatives, as the media portrays it as well, believe it is a stupid gaffe, it is not, it is an underhanded way of threatening the population with something that is not true and could not be true, but is so blatantly repugnant, that people will think of its possibility, thereby planting a seed thought of racism against the Romney campaign. This is one way racism seed thoughts get planted. This was not a gaffe. It may, or may not have been a carefully scripted plan, but no matter the event of VP Biden opening his mouth, he and President Obama have agreed that he is the clown of the constituency and he wears that badge with pride.

Hence, Biden is made to say a 'gaffe', sound like a buffoon, but makes his social liberal point of divisiveness all the same. His words are being replicated thousands and thousands of times over since they have been spoken, to the point, where, if it were possible, everyone on the planet earth will have heard them. Any politician would love that opportunity. This is not that deep.

The art of social liberal propaganda is not that deep either, however, it has been so successful in the past, it has to use such tactics, again, in order to replicate itself. The seed gets planted by the dumb farmer, so to speak, and then it is watered, and fertilized, by its replicators, with me being one of them.

If I tell you the truth, are you able to listen? If someone else tells you a lie, do you know the difference? The propagandist is betting on your ignorance and all who follow the social liberal ideology have a belief system that will not allow them to think, or believe their way out of it.

There is, however, an exception to the former statement, and the exception is this: the way out of a social liberal thought belief system is what I term as, "a moment of revision". The moment of revision is when a person instantaneously changes their mind about something quite profound to their belief system due to an inadvertent, or purposeful, action or word. Their course is changed precipitously from one belief to another, or, at times, simply not knowing what to believe, but knowing that they have been lied to and manipulated and now know for certain that they can no longer believe the propaganda of the social liberal. This is the change of being in the parable of the prodigal son...he came to his senses.

The moment of revision is a transaction of thought into will. It is because of this moment of revision that it is so vital that truth be relayed in such a manner as to be right and true and kind. Or, call it professional, but it must be the truth, spoken in truth, because people do not understand holy love, because we really do not understand a Holy God.

The Dissolution of Truth

For My thoughts are not your thoughts, nor are your ways My ways, Says the Lord. For as the heavens are higher than the earth, so are My ways higher than your ways, and My thoughts than your thoughts.   (Isaiah 55:8-9)

Understand you senseless among the people;

And you fools, when will you be wise?

He who planted the ear, shall He not hear?

He who formed the eye, shall He not see?

He who instructs the nations, shall He not correct?

He who teaches man knowledge?

The Lord knows the thoughts of a man,

That they are futile.

Blessed is the man whom You instruct, O Lord.

And teach out of Your law.

That You may give him rest from the days of adversity,

Until the pit is dug for the wicked.

For the Lord will not cast off His people.

Nor will He forsake His inheritance,

But judgment will return to righteousness,

And all the upright in heart will follow it.   (Psalm 94:8-15)

It is to the moment of revision that I pray for our countrymen, to see that it is the Lord Who has provided a way for us to follow. It is to my dying breath that the citizens of the United States of America begin to follow the Creator of itself, the Lord God Almighty, for His glory and not to the glory of men.

Terry Lursen

Amendment I of the United States Constitution

Amendment I of the United States Constitution states:

Congress shall make no law respecting an establishment of religion, or prohibiting the free exercise thereof; or abridging the freedom of speech, or of the press, or of the right of the people peaceably to assemble, and to petition the government for a redress of grievances.

The points made in earlier years by the progressive liberal agenda have become evermore egregious to the populace of the United States of America. The liberal agenda has become ever increasingly socialistic and dictatorial in its make-up, thought, and coercive actions to thwart any kind of religion from operating freely within these United States.

There is absolutely no support for the 'separation of church and state' interpretations set forthwith by the liberal agenda.

There is absolutely no support for the idea of 'freedom from religion' interpretations set forthwith by the liberal agenda.

As I have stated earlier in my writings, these predisposed ideologies are purely reflexive in nature causing themselves to believe themselves for what they believe; they believe unto themselves for their own personal edification and the for the ultimate control of others and their destiny. Their main premise of operation is control by any means necessary and a lie told by liars will do any day.

The Dissolution of Truth

The current operations and actions performed by the liberal agenda to create their own interpretations as rule of law and decree reveal the ignorance of the masses as to the true rule of law as set forth in the Constitution of the United States of America. It simply does not say what they say it says. They interpret simplicity and misconstrue the writings and the nature of our constitution. The idea of separation of church and state is not in the Constitution of the United States of America, nor is it implied. That idea was presented by Thomas Jefferson in a letter to the Danbury Baptist Association in 1802 presenting the idea of protecting the church from the government, as in 'a wall of separation between church and state'. President Jefferson was explaining the law to them as to reassure them of their protection from infringement from the government. Excerpts from the letter are as follows:

"Believing with you that religion is a matter which lies solely between a man and his God, that he owes no account to none other for his faith or his worship, that the legislative powers of government reach actions only, and not opinions, I contemplate with sovereign reverence that act of the whole American people which declared that their legislature should "make no law respecting an establishment of religion, or prohibiting the free exercise thereof," thus building a wall of separation between church and State. Adhering to this expression of the supreme will of the nation in behalf of the rights of conscience, I shall see with sincere satisfaction the progress of those sentiments which tend to restore to man all his natural rights, convinced he has no natural right in opposition to his social duties.

I reciprocate your kind prayers for the protection and blessing of the common Father and Creator of man, and tender you for yourselves and your religious association, assurances of my high respect and esteem." [1]

In this letter, there is no mention of separation of religion from the people, nor is there any idea of setting forth a rule of law stating that religion must be compartmentalized to protect the government and its people. In any case, the interpretations of this letter are mute, they are not the law, nor were they intended to be; it was a kind letter sent to President Jefferson's constituents for their edification, explanation, and protection. The letter is the exact opposite of what the liberal, socialistic agenda proposes that the law states.

In no way can an organization set forth a grievance against a person for his involvement with a religious organization, whether that person be a business owner, an independent contractor, employee of a business or an employee of a state, or federal institution. The persons of the United States of America are protected under Amendment I to participate freely in their right to religion and religious exercise.

It is to the distress of the liberal thought that they take offence at religion, particularly Christianity, born of Jesus Christ, and this offence is the stumbling block of their ideology. They are not free, they are held in bondage to their ideology and are hid together with bonds that cannot be broken without the saving grace of that which they have purposed to destroy. Their destiny is in their purpose of destruction. Any and all organizations affiliated with the liberal ideology are culpable constrictors of all faith based organizations and it is to this battle that they have created that their demise is imminent.

There is no rule of law stating a separation of church and state. It is a myth perpetuated by groups like the freedom from religion founda-

The Dissolution of Truth

tion who desire to have a society free from religion and they intend to force as many people as they can to believe their ideologies. Their latest attempt is to try and stop a Georgia high school football team and their coach from having their meals served by the local churches.

The law of the constitution has not changed, what has changed is the darkness of these human souls, at any and all cost, to, not only prevent the cause of religion to progress, but to exterminate it from our country and are attempting to use the ignorance of the populace to do it.

Enough is now.

Terry Lursen

Obama's Evisceration of God from the Populace

The social liberal cannot have any god in its path in order for true complicity to proceed. The obvious trial of the iniquitous regime during the democrat's convention proved its fallibility in its efforts to quench any thought or mention of God from their pulpit. The platform was set, but the ever stalwart leadership of the current Republican Party saw through the guise and intervened with such fervor that not even Obama could stand the heat of Truth bearing down on him. He acted as though he had nothing to do with the democrats outlawing of the mention of His Name, which if he didn't have anything to do with it, it once again resonates the inability and the incompetence of the not-a-leader. If he did have knowledge of the evisceration of the mention of His Name, then he is indubitably the undermining of all that we as a nation profess and that is, "In God We Trust'.

The shifting of sands of the social liberal denotes that the adjustments have to be made in order to win the election; they have to win in order for their plan of removing religion from this nation. They have to win in order to proceed with the agenda of propagating ideology that is totally incongruous with Judeo-Christian thought. They have to win in order to pay back the folk who have ordered their success. They have to win in order to bring about change of the iniquitous design: the sodomites, the necromancers, the law changers,

The Dissolution of Truth

and the truth creators. Obama's evisceration of God from our nation was tried at his convention, and battled for unsuccessfully because not everyone believes what he believes.

He believes in the government governing totally. His absolute authority is challenging even the best of his cronies. He wants what she wants and she wants what the other she wants. He must disengage anything that stands in his way and remove it from his eyes and ours as well. He can have no other god before him. He promises the people that he will take from the rich and give it to the poor; when, in actuality, he will take from everyone as much as he can and give it away, because that's what social liberals do. It's like the bank robber who has just robbed the bank and is driving recklessly down the street throwing the money out the window that he just took from the bank. Besides, it's not his money anyway.

Again, not everyone believes what he believes, especially in his own party. In God we trust, indeed. For it was God Who brought forth this nation. It was God who led people here for His purposes and they survived through the years of disease, famine, terror, and lack. It has been God Who has protected us through the years and it has been God Who has been our provider. The battles have been won because of God and it is to God's glory that we are still here as a nation in spite of the lack of leadership that prevails in our nation today. The unwitting believe that they can remove God and religion from our midst in order that they may have their way cleared for their own selfish desires. Remove what you think you need to remove but know this: the Kingdom of God does not come with observation, but is within every Spirit-filled believer. You cannot remove what you cannot see. The Kingdom of God will not be eviscerated...ever.

Church and State

The calling of a man of God does not come from the populace. It is not voted upon by any group of people, nor is it bequeathed upon a man by any other man or woman. The calling of a man of God is exactly that, a calling of and from the One True God, in the book of the Revelation, His name is Jesus Christ.

The God of the Bible is the God of the Genesis through the Revelation. He is the God of yesterday, today, and tomorrow. He is the God of Abraham, Moses, Elijah; He is the God of the Hebrew people. His name is Yahweh, Adonai, Savior, Redeemer, Jehovah, Creator, and Lord. The Lord, our God, is One. There is one Lord, one faith, one baptism. He is the King of the kings and the Lord of the lords. He created all things and without Him, nothing was made. He made the heavens and the earth and all that have dwelt upon the earth, including you and me. The New Testament calls the Christ Jesus, Lord and Savior.

He is the God of love and the God of judgment. Righteousness is in His right hand and with mercy and loving kindness He reigns supremely over all that is. He is Savior in that He has provided a way of escape for all of us, from the consequences of sin, into Himself through the saving grace in the blood atonement of Jesus Christ. He is all of this and He is forever more than we could ever imagine.

It is what is in the heart, after all, that the man of God has to use from his own personal experience to the hearts of the many who

The Dissolution of Truth

need a Savior. When man takes critical judgment upon himself to judge another man, he has taken the duty and righteousness of a just and holy God upon himself as the ruler over another man's soul. As humans, the word of God speaks very plainly, that is not our right, it is the right of a just, righteous, and holy God. That is why He said, "... do not to give what is holy to the dogs; nor cast your pearls before swine, lest they trample them under your feet, and turn and tear you in pieces." (Matthew 7:6). Righteous judgment is for a right judge. There is one true judge and that is God Himself. When humans take the judgment of others upon themselves, they tear other people up with their words and their flesh as dogs would with a defenseless creature condemning others to a fate that they themselves think they are above and are not. God, alone, is judge, His judgments are just and right.

Confusion and degradation comes in now and says that we cannot discern right from wrong, or know sin from righteousness. What I am saying is that we do not have the right to condemn people to hell. We can tell them what we believe to be the Biblical truth and then they have the final say with the help of the Holy Spirit, or not. One of the reasons the world looks at the church's message with resentment is that they receive it in a spirit of condemnation rather than holy love. The main reason the world looks at the church with resentment, however, is that the world simply doesn't want to be told what to do about their personal sin.

This brings us to another problem and that is the cause of the world that certain individuals and groups would have against the church and that the church should not be involved in politics. These are the people who have traded truth for a lie and have regarded themselves as little gods of their own domain and have left the God of the Bible for their own selfishness, entertainment, sports, political gods, money, addictions, and the list is endless as to what a person who does not want to hear about God can get themselves involved in.

These are the people who have believed the lie that there are laws concerning the separation of church and state. There is no such law in the Constitution of the United States, however, liberal ideologists have created the lie that there is and so, in the last 60 years these liberal thinkers have been able to persuade the uninformed to change federal, state, and local governmental policy which is contrary to the US Constitution. These people do not want God in anything, especially if it has to do with anything concerning the government, federal, state, or local, schools, sports, prayer, or Biblical teaching.

Amendment I of the Constitution reads:

Congress shall make no law respecting an establishment of religion, or prohibiting the free exercise thereof; or abridging the freedom of speech, or of the press; or the right of the people peaceably to assemble, and to petition the Government for a redress of grievances.

There is no law of separation of church and state, it is a lie and only an abuse of words from Thomas Jefferson's letter to the Danbury Baptists. And, because people have been raised by a lie and have separated themselves from a Holy God, they do not want a religious person telling them what to do with the government. They want the political to be kept free from the religious. It was not so in the beginning. God is in all things. God has always been in all things. He is in the very breath that you breathe.

The Dissolution of Truth

Our forefathers have their writings taken out of context to try and prove the antithesis of agreement with our Creator. The proof of their agreement with our Creator is all over our nation, in their writings, and most especially in the halls of our federal buildings. Truth is written in the halls, the mantels, the walls, the doorposts, inside and out. Go to Washington, DC, yourself and see the liberty that was purchased for you and me with the blood of men and the assurance of their faith sketched into the granite, the marble, the wood, and the artwork. Go to the Library of Congress and see the Bibles that we have stored there for public viewing. There are museums there, but the word of God is not for a museum just to observe, it is proof that our forefathers loved, read, respected, and adored the word of God. Go and see for yourself that it was the Lord God who made us a nation and great men who followed and served a Mighty God. These men were farmers, soldiers, politicians, writers, industrialists, entrepreneurs, and on and on, and they had the faith in a just and holy God to deliver us as a nation to prosper us as He saw fit. Our trust is in God.

It is right and just that a man of God speak to the good and the ills of our nation. It is right and just for a man of God to speak for if that man is not allowed to speak, then who is allowed to speak? What spirit shall prevail if the man of God is not allowed to speak to the political?

It is right and just for men of God to speak to the political and to every area of life. It is right and just for the man of God to continue in his calling because it was God who called him to the task of preaching truth and he will not answer to me or to you, he will answer to his God who is my God as well.

Terry Lursen

The Egregious Moment

While driving through a busy shopping center today on my way to the grocery store, the vehicles were moving quite slow because of all the cars maneuvering around the pedestrians. I was driving and as I looked to my right, walking along the sidewalk in front of the stores, I glanced to see in a quick moment, a dad punched his son in the stomach. My vehicle was stopped as a result of the traffic and the pit bull in my front seat and I gave the dad a glaring stare. We had caught him in the act.

The son, about 14 years old, was afraid. His hands were in a forward position as to protect himself, but it was on his face...fear. Fear was not only on his face, it was in his arms and hands for they were crimpled with no energy to create a fist to protect himself. The boy walked in silence, with separation now between him and his dad.

The dad had immediately turned to look my way to see if anyone had seen him do what he did. From the disposition of the trembling son, this was not the first time. The dad knew I saw him as he proceeded briskly along the sidewalk.

In the moment, in the ever egregious moment, I watched the dad move on with the son in a weakened state behind him. The boy was in an arthritic condition of arrested fear. They moved on as I did in my car out of sight. Was this the first time? Why did the dad treat him so? Does the dad not know he has made him as he is?

The Dissolution of Truth

How we treat our children is reflected in their faces as a mirror of time and space reflects all things. All things are seen and heard in moments of joy and laughter, tears and regret.

Treat your children well. Love them with hugs and words of inspiration. Smile a smile away and smile once more and see the child in need. Their tears are removed by your presence; not only your children, but the children of the world who truly need love and kindness and the protection of the Almighty.

The Immoral Leader

There once was a man of sin
He went to his bed and back again.
To live his life as he chose fit;
Living in life, he chose death.
He's lived in the world all his life,
Whatever he chose, his choice was right.
His mind, he believed in his cause for sure;
With pride of mind, his soul endured.
With sex and pleasure, his heart did stay.
No belief in wrong, there's no hell to pay.
In his mind, he is right and that all the time;
With pride of life, his soul doth pine.
There is no wrong unless you tell.
"You condemn, you preach, you talk of hell."
In his mind he is right, that man of sin;

Terry Lursen

To go to his bed and back again.

He is the president, some men say;

Still others hope for another day.

But this man of sin, he lives for self;

He boasts of lies, his pride remains.

This man of sin with pride in hand

Leads others to believe his belief is grand.

"No wrong," says he for all is well.

He believes in heaven, but not in hell.

"Do what you want, for all is right!"

"Lie with the beast in your bed tonight."

He does not see, nor does he care;

To sleep with whomever, no doors to bear.

There is no right, there is no wrong.

In his mind, he lives the whole day long.

This selfish pawn leads others astray

He does not believe in hell to pay.

To equal cause and equal rights:

"Lie with the beast in your bed tonight!"

"I own the land!" He says with glee;

"Be the immoral, your soul shall be free.

"Your soul set free to do as you please."

In his mind he has done, it is his destiny.

To free the beast, he has done his part;

This man of sin; immoral in heart.

Homosexuality and Christianity

Christianity and that, being a Christian, means one who is fully devoted to Jesus Christ. Being a Christian, according to Jesus Christ, is one who has repented of their sins, believed in faith the work of Jesus Christ on the cross, has been born again into newness of life, has become a new creation in Christ, and is following Him in love and obedience to His commands. One would have to quote the majority of the New Testament as its proof of these statements for it is in these statements that becoming a Christian is its foundation.

To say that a human could be both a homosexual and a Christian is the epitome of oxymoron, that of combining two contradictory or incongruous terms.

Taking a look at homosexuality is to take a look at what it really is. Homosexuality, in this particular context, is where a male has chosen to have sexual relations with another male, or, a female has chosen to have sexual relations with another female. The natural state of man to have sexual relations, according to the Biblical view of marriage, is "Therefore a man shall leave his father and mother and be joined to his wife, and they shall become one flesh." (Genesis 2:24) Anyone having a sexual relationship outside of this Biblical marriage view would be considered committing fornication.

Fornication is having a sexual relation with another person outside of marriage. If a person is married and that person has a sexual relationship with another person who is not their spouse; that is called adultery. Both fornication and adultery are sins in the eyes of God. Not only is fornication and adultery unlawful in the eyes of God, they are unnatural in the sense of peace among the married because sexual intercourse is a joining of the body, mind and soul. It is a sense of becoming one with another. It is naturally unacceptable for a married man to have an adulterous relationship with another woman who is not his wife. It is betrayal and the act of being unfaithful on the part of the one who commits the adulterous act.

One of the disturbing aspects of the homosexual agenda is that there is a belief in not believing that Biblical view of marriage. The Biblical view of marriage is. It not only 'is', it is a faith fact. If a person becomes a Christian, then they have declared and confessed Jesus as Lord. If they do so, they do so in faith. It is irrefutable. Another person cannot come up to the Christian and say they are not a Christian just because they said they are not. Being a Christian is faith-based and because it is faith-based, it is adhered to in faith. It is the work of God. The commandments of our Lord are real and true and we Christians believe that as a faith fact. Just because someone else doesn't believe the faith facts of the scripture, it doesn't mean that they are not real and true, or that they do not exist, because they do; that person simply does not believe in the Bible.

In this regard, everything that I am writing here is based on the scriptures, and I personally believe in the totality of the scriptures; they are the Word of God and they are wholly holy inspired and true. Jesus said that He is the way, the truth and the life and I believe all of that. I have also given my life to Him in humble obedience in response

The Dissolution of Truth

to His love and forgiveness. Does that mean that I am holy and without sin, of course not. What it does mean is that Jesus' holiness and righteousness has become my righteousness and I am able to enter into His righteousness by His atoning work on the cross. I am forgiven. I have left my old ways behind.

So, if a person says that they do not adhere to the Biblical view of marriage, they simply do not believe in the Word of God. They do not believe in what is God-made, natural, and the fact that we are made in His image. It is ok not to believe God, however, there are consequences to adverse beliefs against God as Paul states.

Romans 1:24-32 says:

Therefore God also gave them up to uncleanness, in the lusts of their hearts, to dishonor their bodies among themselves, who exchanged the truth of God for a lie, and worshipped and served the creature rather than the Creator, who is blessed forever. Amen. For this reason, God gave them up to vile passions. For even their women exchanged the natural use for what is against nature. Likewise also the men, leaving the natural use of the woman, burned in their lust for one another, men with men committing what is shameful, and receiving in themselves the penalty of their error which was due. And even as they did not like to retain God in their knowledge, God gave them over to a debased mind, to do those things which are not fitting; being filled with all unrighteousness, sexual immorality, wickedness, covetousness, maliciousness; full of envy, murder, strife, deceit, evil-mindedness; they are whisperers, backbiters, haters of God, violent, proud, boasters, inventors of evil things, disobedient to parents, undiscerning, untrustworthy, unloving, unforgiving, unmerciful; who, knowing the righteous judgment of God, that those who practice such things are deserving of death, not only do the same but also approve of those who practice them.

This passage of scripture is very clear in that man's passion for another man or a woman's passion for another woman is sexually immoral and wicked. It is deserving of death. But, some say, what about the adulterer? The same is true, it is sexually immoral and wicked. Sex outside of marriage is unlawful.

Jesus said that even if a man looked upon a woman with lust in his heart, he had committed adultery with her. (Matthew 5:28). What is it, though, that makes a man or woman, an adulterer versus committing an act of adultery? Is it that one act of thought? Is it that one, or even many acts of being with someone outside of the marriage? What makes a person a homosexual? It is not God, for it is a choice to sin. Is it permanent and eternal? If you had sex with someone before you got married, are you eternally damned as a result of your fornication?

1 Corinthians 6:9-11 says:

Do you not know that the unrighteous will not inherit the kingdom of God? Do not be deceived. Neither fornicators, nor idolaters, nor adulterers, nor homosexuals, nor sodomites, nor thieves, nor covetous, nor drunkards, nor revilers, nor extortioners will inherit the kingdom of God. And such were some of you. But you were washed, but you were sanctified, but you were justified in the name of the Lord Jesus and by the Spirit of our God.

A key word in this passage is the word, 'were'. 'And such were some of you…' Here we see that, yes, a person can sin, the sin of adul-

The Dissolution of Truth

tery or the sin of homosexuality and, yet, still become a born again believer in Jesus Christ in that they are made new in Him. It is the atoning blood of Jesus Christ that 'washes', and it is by His grace that we can become sanctified and justified in Him. However, the lifestyle has to be left behind. If there is a real, true and faithful born again experience, the lifestyle will be left behind. If not, then it is plausible to doubt there ever was a real change and the person is not a true disciple of Jesus Christ. They just think they are as a result of errant teaching, a wrong belief system or wishful thinking.

In Romans 2:7, Paul talks about '...eternal life to those by patient continuance in doing good seek for glory, honor and immortality; but for those who are self-seeking and do not obey the truth, but obey unrighteousness, indignation and wrath, tribulation and anguish, on every soul of man who does evil to the Jew first and also to the Greek."

Another key here is when Paul talks about the 'faithful continuance'. One has to ponder if there are so many sins against God, who, then, could be saved? But it is through God's grace that men are saved, not of any work, it is the grace of God. God's grace is far greater than any man could ever imagine and yet His righteous judgment is sure and just. He will do what He has said He will do.

It is in our lives that we not only say we are Christian, a follower and disciple of Jesus Christ, but that we leave behind that which he saved us from, that being our sin. We then follow Him in faithful continuance into eternal life.

If a person chooses to faithfully continue in their adultery, their homosexuality, or their fornication, they are sure to meet a certain eternal death. The Word of God is clear. It all has to be and will be left behind if there has been true repentance and a true change of heart born only by the Holy Spirit of God.

"Therefore if anyone is in Christ, he is a new creation; old things have passed away; behold, all things have become new." (2 Corinthians 5:17, NKJV).

"Jesus answered and said to him, 'Most assuredly, I say to you, unless one is born again, he cannot see the kingdom of God." (John 3:3, NKJV)

"For God did not send His Son into the world to condemn the world, but that the world through Him might be saved. He who believes in Him is not condemned; but he who does not believe is condemned already, because he has not believed in the name of the only begotten Son of God. And this is the condemnation, that the light has come into the world, and men loved darkness rather than light, because their deeds were evil. For everyone practicing evil hates the light and does not come into the light, lest his deeds should be exposed. But he who does the truth comes to the light, that his deeds may be clearly seen, that they have been done in God." (John 3:17-21, NKJV)

There is forgiveness and hope for the homosexual, the adulterer and the fornicator, to leave their lifestyle and walk in the Light of God. It is their only hope.

And so it is written that truth be revealed and that truth be an opportunity to be believed. Paul says in Romans 2, not to judge, just as Jesus Christ implored us not to judge others. Therefore there is no judgment here.

The popular argument of the homosexual agenda is that if anything is said against their beliefs, then it is 'hatred, bigotry, or closed-mindedness'. It is said that they will not tolerate anything said against them in any regard. Their views are their views and are not the truth. These particular views that if anything is said against their views, then it is hatred or a lack of tolerance, when by their very words, they are intolerant of any adverse view, which by the mirror spoken makes that viewpoint the viewpoint of a bigot.

It is also said that if their views are not agreed with, then the opposing view is disrespecting them and condemning them, therefore the opposing view is said to be unloving. It is ironic and hypocritical that the homosexual who clearly does not respect anyone's views save the views of agreement with their philosophies thereby calling the opposing view disrespectful.

It is the same as one person seeing another person heading off a cliff to their death and demise and warns the person of the imminent danger that is about to occur, but the person heading off the cliff responds with, "You hater, why are you disrespecting me? I know what I'm doing!" That would be a ridiculously haughty response to someone who knows what is about to happen and trying to save someone from death and yet the person heading off the cliff feels infringed upon and says that they are being treated as un-equals.

It is true that we reap what we sow. If the viewpoint is to vehemently attack anyone with an adverse view that they are filled with hate, then the mirror displays what is in the mirror. So it is with intolerance and bigotry. To not tolerate another's view is intolerance, whether it is the Christian's view or the homosexual viewpoint. Human depravity knows no bounds.

If a homosexual has a viewpoint different than presented here, the difference lies not in Biblical interpretation, but in an argument with God. God has spoken. God is just and only He is the judge. His Word is real and true. It is heard in the Spirit so it is not surprising when the adverse is spoken against God and His word because they simply do not hear it nor do they understand it.

And just as Jesus forgave the woman caught in the act of adultery, He said to her, "Neither do I condemn you; go, and sin no more." (John 8:10). I stand as no one's judge, but as a proclaimer of truth to the nations, "Go, and sin no more."

If the homosexual decides to live his or her life in homosexual acts and behaviors, then it is their clear choice to do so. In no way can they claim themselves 'born again', or 'a new creation in Christ' until the Holy Spirit works in their lives and they actually become born again and leave the life behind that they claim they are and allow the Holy Spirit's power to work a work in their lives unlike they have never seen before.

Paul said in Romans 8:1, "Therefore there is no condemnation to those who are in Christ Jesus, who do not walk according to the flesh, but according to the spirit." (NKJV) This is for the believer who is 'in Christ Jesus'. Otherwise, the condemnation remains by a person's own choices. God does not make a person commit homosexual acts, nor has He made any human a homosexual of Divine origin; it is their choice. The behaviors are learned just as any other behavior that walks in its own way and not the ways of God.

The Dissolution of Truth

"For if you live according to the flesh, you will die; but if by the Spirit you put to death the deeds of the body, you will live." (Romans 8:13)

"I call heaven and earth as witnesses today against you, that I have set before you life and death, blessing and cursing; therefore choose life, that both you and your descendants may live; that you may love the Lord your God, that you may obey His voice, and that you may cling to Him, for He is your life and the length of your days..." (Deuteronomy 30:19-20a, NKJV)

Terry Lursen

The Philosophy of the Gilded Mind

As it has come to the attention of the historian, philosophy and history are prone to repeat themselves in spaces and lines of regurgitated redundancy, so that in most instances one might call the repeated ideas and events a theft if it weren't for so many minutes and miles in between. But for the gilded mindset, there is often no regret, nor adherence to any former things, for in the mind of the gilded, originality is brewed instantaneously upon request and thought to be the order of the mind of the great, but is only a vain repetition of the past.

Golden hues and heavy golden molts are not always one and the same. Real gold is weighty and progressively expensive to the mainstream and yet to the novice who does not care for the matter, real gold is that which is beholden to the fanciful dreamer; it is the financier of all things tangible and wealthy. Real gold is known as a true substance and knows no bounds to its global notoriety.

Gildedness, however, has almost been around for as long as the real thing. To gild an object is to give the object of far less value an appearance of attractiveness and make it to seem real in golden hue and color. Gilded objects are covered with a thin layer of gold, or painted gold, to give that appearance of the real thing. It is to give a deceptively attractive or improved appearance that conceals something of little worth. (The FreeDictionary.com). Substitutionary measures always take place when the real thing is not available.

The Dissolution of Truth

Thus we have in our day a broad stroke of gilded proportions the vain repetition of that which was and has been and is absolutely nothing new. That being, the current President of the United States, one who has been gifted the opportunity to lead this great nation to move forward in prosperity but is, after all, himself gilded in all his glory to the end of this age and forevermore in his mind.

This gilded minded man is consistent with himself and predictable to the extent that if there is anything of worth to this nation at any given time, it will simply have to wait on him. Placated aromas of golden halos hover amidst the whereabouts of the one's so consumed with themselves that the world is their cup of opportunity and they drink it ever so slowly at the expense of the American people. Personal philosophies and beliefs abound to these people of renown so much so that there is no wonder at where the gavel will be pronounced, it's just a matter of when.

He sees his second portion as a continuance of a gift gifted to the holy, for in him there is no amount of fault or accountability, only the transference of blame and that in due time for every event held in his office. Perfection to the gilded mind is attainable and non-transferable. Personal absorption of imbued improprieties are inconsequential for the gilded mind is above all and sees all in the mirror of the fairest of them all.

The philosophy of the gilded mind is one of intense internal self-relegated perception that there is no other than his own personal beliefs to be expounded upon. Self-aggrandizement is his mantra and the pursuit of all things considered progressive is his pen. He is chief interpreter of the Constitution of the United States. He knows all, sees all, understands all and for the *piece de resistance*, he is committed only to his interpretations of that which has been sanctified in his mind. To him, his gilded halo is real, for everything he has touched has turned to his version of gold. Albeit, gilded, because he thinks his version of gold is real.

The philosophy of the gilded mind is personal perspective endeavoring to change all that is to itself. After all, what the world has done to itself thus far is deplorable and it has been waiting impatiently for this gilded gift to arrive on the scene to save the world from itself to this man's personal truth. All must be followers of the way for the way is the way of true life in him and it doesn't matter if you think him wrong for his beliefs for he is getting paid handsomely in fame, fortune, authority and eternal security with his father and lord.

One example of him being the immoral leader is funding the immorality of the homosexual agenda with his authority and curious thoughts of his past. He believes in homosexuality and homosexual marriage as a formidable way of life. He sees no harm in their endeavors and vows to make the populace of the United States in agreement with his/their ideology. They are in agreement. What it is they have agreed upon is up for discussion, however. What is it truly that drives a certain man to perpetuate the belief system of the homosexual agenda? He says it's about equality, so if it's about equality, then why does he not take up the cause of the adulterer as well? Again, what drives a certain man to perpetuate a way of life if not for the life itself to be desired to be lived out personally? Has anyone asked him that question?

Reflexivity is abundant in this domain. The gilded mind thrives upon its belief system and in a rather demure manner expunges any other belief other than its own. Internalities prey upon other souls.

The Dissolution of Truth

Certainly, if he thinks his truth is the truth, then all should be following his way of thought. The gilded philosophy requires nothing less than the demand of the faithful to be faithful to him and to him alone. Cult leaders are entirely the same. Reflexive reciprocity demands it. And, in his own valiant mind, it must be the will of God for he has heard somewhere that all authority belongs to the One True God who put him in his place of authority. Gilded kings have been abundant throughout time and were used by God for specific purposes to discipline the unfaithful and create the true longing for God that He desired in their hearts. It is no compliment to be awarded the nature of a gilded ruler.

And yet, pride remains. Consumption remains. Spending what is not yours to spend and spending what you do not have is *e'honte'*, literally, shameless. *Abandonne'!*

And for all of this, the American public is ridiculed if his prerogatives are not imbued with the same set of gilded wings as his infallible words set in flight. The reflexive nature of the gilded mind sees only its sight and expects others to see as he sees or be damned. This is the native characteristic of a divisive president. Keep dividing your enemies until they are no more, otherwise, the reflexive domain cannot exist. There is no fear in our enemies' eyes. They are waiting, not for another one of his mistakes, no. They are waiting for the time and the seasons to be completed. He is very much a part of this season of demise. He is playing his part in history.

We have been here before, but not exactly. Time has past, but this time Israel is. A formidable foe and a plethora of pain awaits. Then a real leader will emerge, one that will take the gilded mind to entirely new heights that the world will live to regret.

Terry Lursen

Initializing Freedom

There is within the heart of man, that is, most men, the desire to be free. Most men desire the desire to be free without having to work much at the thought whilst others are completely satisfied within the domain of common existence.

Common existence is that which man finds himself within the usual and customary albeit not many wise and not many free. Intrusiveness of thoughts requiring change from the known are intrusive indeed. Men will fight within their existence to remain unchanged for it is in this place that man finds comfort in his current surroundings. It is a place of receiving and never giving, a place of redundancy and complacency, a place of nether and comfortabilities...the place of kings and paupers of emperors and pawns.

Common existence is that which has been and always will be. It is neither desire nor forbearance nor is it any virtue that plays upon the hearts of men who desire truth. Common existence has no heart to the existential and plays no part to the fruition of any common good. Common existence is merely accepted as a norm and regarded as the way of life in par with no view of sight in view.

The reflexive domain of control whether it is in the sociopolitical realm or the realm of the religious hierarchy demands its way upon the masses through the abhorrent tactic of will demise. The will of man is the most important factor in the constriction and control of another. Common existence, however, has already conquered the human will in past generations so that those who live in the current live presumably unaware of their possibilities. Reflexivity compounds thought upon thought to the unaware as an inbreeding of mind over matter and the leader's mind over all. Religious cults and sociopolitical systems are constructed the same. They are constructed by the decomposition of the human will. It is acted upon by the simultaneous influence of the controller and the degeneration of the mind and will of man.

The will of man is to be broken within the construct of the reflexive domain and when it is found to be broken, education of the children and political propaganda become the primary vehicles of the transmogrification of any society.

To the one man or woman who desires above all to be free even when this person does not clearly understand the concept of freedom, freedom is a voice within the composition of entanglement that is set to deceive and never to relieve. Freedom's voice calls from the deep to be set free even though life and limb be the purest cost of all. The will of man is at its precipice with the price of freedom waiting in the balance. Will the man's will decide its own fate or will it lay down its will at the cost of its own freedom?

For the society of men and women who have been broken by the will of desperate men in ages past and generations of death succumbed, it is time for the will of men to seek that which is in their heart by the design of an Almighty God. It is past time to seek that which cries from the depths of the human soul the cry to be free, the cry to be free.

It is here that the initialization of freedom begins. The here is the heart of men and women who have seen that the power of the will of man is more powerful than any construct of altered human design. Freedom cries to be set free. Free from the tyranny of the mind; free from the tyranny of men; free from the tyranny of the social constructs of the last century.

The reflexive domain of control in society relies upon the common existence of its fellow men and has declared an eternal war of damnation upon the will of man.

Will the will of man initialize its own freedom from this tyranny of control? Will the heart of that which cries in the wilderness to seek a perfect justice be appeased? Is it time to be free from the control of the past to raise the flag of freedom for the children if its future?

The will of man will decide and your children will be the prize.

The Certain Uncertainty of Man

There have been men in certain times who have used and oft repeated words like submission, denial and the Lordship of Jesus Christ. It is not so much anymore. Even many of the church leaders have become pleasers of themselves as well as others in order that they might gain some gain that would be of personal benefit to themselves.

Even still, because most men desire to please themselves, if they feel infringed upon by their right of free thinking, they will go back and attack the men that speak of such things as truth, absolutes, order and submission. The thinking is that "I can be free to think as I please if I denigrate the man that I disagree with. Hence, "I am free to attack the man who speaks about those things that are not of my ideological purpose" (i.e., denial of self, submission, commitment, the Lordship of Jesus Christ and absolute truth).

These attacks are carried out with such vengeance on the character and integrity of honorable men that their words are rendered powerless to those who are of the free thinking persuasion. It is as though there are no honorable men and that is certainly true in the spiritual sense, however, the result is in the plausibility that there is no honorable course of thought because there are no honorable men for all are equal in thought, word and deed. There is only the lesser than the equality denying any greater than. This is geometrically unsound thinking albeit becoming the matter of the many.

Terry Lursen

The free thinker does not debate or do battle with substantiated thought processes based on the foundations of things for the free thinker is able to build his own foundation with his own thoughts and the thoughts of others as he thinks. They corroborate with one another as though the foundations they build are sure and right, but are based on subjective reasoning rather than the absolute of truth, which, in their minds cannot exist, for if it did, their free thinking would be disallowed subsequently forcing submission to the higher thought of the absolute.

In the mind of the free thinker the absolute does not exist because it cannot. If the absolute did exist, their thoughts could not. If their thoughts could not be as they deem them to be, then there would have to be another would they would be subjected to. The free thinker cannot tolerate the absolute so it declares the absolute as intolerable and any who follow the way of the absolute equally intolerable creating the conundrum of the proliferation of tolerance based on intolerance. Therefore, 'to be' in their minds is to be 'self-free', denying the preponderance of the existence of any absolute truth relegating themselves to the authority of the many, the ways, and the ethereal existence of the free.

A free thinker can have knowledge of the Bible through a careful reading of such but deny its power for he cannot know its power for its power is only illuminated by the power of the Holy Spirit of God who inspired every word written therein. There is the plenary verbal inspiration of the scripture that cannot be received by the free thinker therefore he cannot understand the knowledge that he gains from his readings of the scripture because he does not believe in its Author. The word of God is received in faith in Him. Where there is

The Dissolution of Truth

no faith, there is no revelation, nor understanding.

It is to read the Book as any book and to treat its thoughts as any thoughts or ideas of man. Quintessentially, all is equal in the mind of the free thinker, with the exception of the intolerable. Their thoughts are on equal plane regarding the scripture's interpretation and expression. After all, it is a 'good book'. For the free thinker, his thoughts on the Bible are as the Bible and the denial of the absolute becomes an absolute in itself unbeknownst to the free thinking mind.

The free thinker's freedom to think as he pleases relegates the foundations of all things as equal to his own personal thoughts. It is participial thinking, doing and trying all on my own, but is co-signed with the thinking, doing and trying of those who "sensigate" the noise of the absolute to non-existence. It is the many living in the perceived vibrancy of chaos. And, oddly enough, they do not know how they became. They merely are and choose free thinking as the pathway to ohm.

They are the electrons of Drude set on a collision course with each other against the absolute, drifting at random, yet ever-moving at a velocity controlled by the ebb and flow of the angst.

These are men and women drifting and doubting, believing they are going somewhere with all of this, but they do not know where. They act as waves in their free thinking forgetting that even the ocean waves obey the laws of nature in force and tide. The ocean waves have a purpose and a conductor while the free thinker rejects the possibility of being subjected to a Divine Creator who might have some say so in their existence and purpose. Things are even as they have been; there is nothing new under the sun.

Terry Lursen

"The fool has said in his heart, 'There is no God.' They are corrupt. They have done abominable works. There is none who does good. The Lord looks down on the children of men, to see if there are any who understand, who seek God. They have all turned aside, they have together become corrupt; there is none who does good, no, not one." (Psalm 14:1-3, NKJV)

"If any of you lacks wisdom, let him ask of God, who gives to all liberally and without reproach, and it will be given to him. But let him ask in faith, and with no doubting, for he who doubts is like a wave of the sea driven and tossed by the wind. For let not that man suppose that he will receive anything from the Lord; he is a double-minded man, unstable in all his ways." (James 1:5-8, NKJV)

We have come indeed to the age of the certain uncertainty of man. These are men and women who think freely of themselves and of God. They are the men who are right in their own eyes and despise the authority of the Creator.

These are men and women who have become amateurs in all their reasoning for their thoughts are not His thoughts, nor are their ways His ways. Doctors who become amateur prophets in the practice of their medicine who prognosticate the demise of their clients' health based on the power of their minds and the pride of their practice. It is certainly one thing to diagnose the health of a human and it is far another thing to determine their clients' days by their subjective notions of how long they should have left to live out their days. Who is man that has set the number of days for another man?

These are men and women who are amateur healers of the sick who preach their wares to the masses in hopes of gain and glory.

The Dissolution of Truth

These are preachers and evangelists acting as faith-healers, needing no medical degree in order to deliver the physical healing from their spiritual words. The perceptions of the proud who seek their own glory when in false prophecy and touches of the Divine they are disposed to slide a dollar into their pocket for these so-called healings. Freely they may have been given, but with great gain they gratify themselves as doctors of faith. Who are these men and women who wield the faith of our Lord as a magical wand over the ignorance of the poor?

These are the educators who become amateur philosophers teaching students their personal philosophies and beliefs unbeknownst to the child and the parents. They teach the children what to think according to the teacher's personal belief system. And, as C.S. Lewis surmised in "The Abolition of Man", regarding the authors of a youths' textbook, "...It's not a theory they put into his mind, but an assumption, which ten years hence, its origin forgotten and its presence unconscious, will condition him to take one side of a controversy which he has not recognized as a controversy at all...the boy...cannot know what is being done to him."[1]

These are the amateur politicians who control men's lives by the stroke of a pen determining who shall work and make gain, and control the flow of money throughout the countryside according to how they deem wise in their own minds. These are lovers of themselves seeking the proverbial pot of gold at the end of their rainbow at the expense of their countrymen's labors. It is all befitting in these times of uncertainty that the certain uncertainty of men decree their decrees as though they are the gods of their destinies. What man set the sun and the moon in place? What man set the earth in its order around the sun and its order to turn itself about? Does man mind the forces of creation, to set them in place and to be about their business of faithful continuance? Does the mind of man create? Really, does he? Who made you?

The Lord has said, "Who is this who darkens counsel by words without knowledge? Now prepare yourself like a man; I will question you, and you shall answer Me. Where were you when I laid the foundations of the earth? Tell me, if you have understanding, who determined its measurements? Surely you know...have you commanded the morning since your days began, and caused the dawn to know its place, that it might take hold of the ends of the earth? (Job 38:2-4, 12-13a)

As it is with the uncertainty of man, we learn not to depend upon man, but upon the only certain absolute that is and that is our God and Father, through the Lord Jesus Christ.

"Seek the Lord while He may be found, call upon Him while He is near. Let the wicked forsake his way, and the unrighteous man his thoughts; Let him return to the Lord, and He will have mercy on him; and to our God, for He will abundantly pardon. 'For My thoughts are not your thoughts, nor are your ways My ways,' says the Lord. For as the heavens are higher than the earth, so are My ways higher than your ways, and My thoughts than your thoughts." (Is. 55:6-8)

May the righteous and godly men and women everywhere pray; for men's thoughts move upon the earth seeking whom they may conquer to turn yet another child to their way of thinking. It is past time that the prayers of the righteous be heard before an Almighty God. The time to pray and move is now.

Abortion Is Murder

"Then He will answer them, saying, 'Truly I say to you, to the extent that you did not do it to the least of these, you did not do it to Me.' And these will go away into eternal punishment, but the righteousness into eternal life." (Matthew 25:45-46)

When the righteous exercise the faith that they have been given by Jesus Christ, they exercise it in allowing Him to have His way in them. Faith comes from the Holy Spirit of God; it is not something conjured up within ourselves. Faith exercised is faith shared out of the overflow of the Spirit within us to a world of opportunities that are constantly around us. Faith exercised is feeding the hungry and giving drink to the thirsty. Faith exercised is visiting the sick and the imprisoned, but this is not mere social service, but a Spirit-filled, Spirit-led opportunity to help others in Jesus' nature. He healed, He delivered, and He fed others in the nature of His Father for it is His nature to feed, give drink, and visit the sick and the imprisoned. Faith in Christ is the Spirit doing His work through us to a lost and hurting world.

The goats, the ones on His left, were the ones when given opportunity turned their face towards another way in order not to see the need. Here, we see that the eternal punishment is for the ones who refuse to help in times of need. But, is that the reason for the eternal punishment? Just because you didn't help in times of need? Emphatically, no! The reason Jesus tells us this parable of the sheep and the goats is that only He knows what is inside a man or woman. He knows if the seed of faith, which is Himself, is living on the inside of that person. If the seed of faith, the Word in the flesh is there, the evidence will be a life lived in the will and nature of the Father. In this, the needy will be seen and helped. The adverse is positively true as well. If a person does not have the faith of God living on the inside of them, then it simply won't matter. The evidence will be there...they will not help the least of these. Ultimately, the goat-spirited person will be helping themselves for themselves.

Social needs have always been with us. Even Jesus told His disciples that the poor you would always have with you. (Matthew 26:11). As a faith-filled disciple, we are admonished to help the needy when we are given opportunity. However, when a person decides that their helping the needy according to their own belief system includes helping women have abortions so that they can murder their unborn babies, the insides of the goat is open for the world to see. People invariably reveal what is on the inside of them. If you really believe that feeding a helpless, homeless dog with one hand and killing an unborn baby with the other hand is your way of social justice or your form of Christian thinking, then I challenge you to read the Word of God in where you will end up with that belief. Abortion is murdering unborn babies and all those who have played their part in the furtherance of this despicable act are just as responsible as the mother herself.

"Jesus said, 'Truly I say to you, to the extent that you did not do it to the least of these, you did not do it to Me.' And these will go away to eternal punishment." (Matt. 25:45-46a)

The Parable of the Indiscernible Palate

Sometimes there are folk who grow up with bad food all of their lives and all they're comfortable with is bad tasting or poorly prepared food. It's like someone who endured their mother or father's terrible cooking and so they cook the same, or worse, then, they feed it to their children...thinking that this is how it's supposed to be and the children learn to be unable to discern the difference between good tasting food and really bad food.

For myself, I keep trying to get it right with my cooking and food preparation for sometimes it's great and other times, well...I can readily admit when I've struck out trying to prepare a really tasty and wholesome meal.

My wife and I will periodically watch food shows on television, some from around the world. We learn secrets from foreign lands, near and far and how they use different seasonings and the variety of ways to prepare delicacies indigenous to their particular culture and upbringing.

I've discovered that the best cooks who seem to really know what they're doing aren't pretentious nor glamorous or pretty. They simply have the taste buds for what is right and good and know how to use quality products with the right ingredients and the perfect amount of seasonings that suits them and the folk that they are preparing the food for.

People who lack a discernible palate will decimate good quality ingredients with the wrong seasoning, improper handling, under-cooking or over-cooking...and, what's worse, they don't even know what they've done wrong or even that they've done anything wrong to make the food taste bad. Bad food just tastes the same to them. The indiscernible palate will make the good bad in order to have what they're used to and most comfortable with; that is, bad food. Furthermore, their children will grow up with the same indiscernible palate, oftentimes repeating the same process by teaching others to do the same...make bad food and eat it, thinking that it's good, or thinking that this is how it's supposed to be, so why complain.

Even still, there are others who think they know good food when they taste it because they have partaken of fine delicacies and great quality food. These folk strive to work and busy their lives in order to purchase richly prepared dinners. Somehow, they believe that because of their income level, they deserve to eat the best; they certainly do not know how it's prepared, and they really don't care, because their finances afford them the luxury of lavish meals at any cost. It is their finances that give them the illusion that they have a finely established palate discernible to the richest of tastes, when in truth, the discernible palate for that which is good doesn't really cost anything but the ability to know that good is good and bad is bad and there is no fine line in-between the two.

A person knows good food and recognizes it, or they don't. It's what's inside the person that discerns the good from the bad and that doesn't cost a dime.

The Author of Marriage

Praying for right thinking...praying for eternal thinking...for holiness... in our nation begins in the home.

Are our personal secrets keeping us from praying for holiness in our nation, holiness in the White House, holiness in the Supreme Court? Can, or will, the fervent prayer of a righteous man see the change in our nation that only God in Jesus Christ can bring about?

There is an absolute Truth, His Name is Jesus Christ.

The idea of marriage is a God idea as it is in the Word of God that marriage is a covenant between a man and a woman. If the idea be described by definition as much as it is described by reality, then any other assessment or re-defining of the idea is corrupt.

Let holy men and women pray for our Supreme Court justices in this season that the Truth of our Lord be reasonable thinking and that the marriage bed be undefiled. Marriage is a holy covenant between a man and a woman. It is.

Terry Lursen

The Consequence of Corruption

Is there anyone who will champion the cause of the child? The swirling, cyclical nature of the procreatic reflexivity relegates itself to itself and the child watches in hunger as the old live in existences of what could have been. What is in man that drives him to the more? Is it mere pride? Is it selfish greed that is so selfish that it entices itself with a total disregard of any consequence? I have been there, a hell-bent puppet guided by my own desires. Is that where we are going as a nation? Will we ever learn from our history and from our mistakes?

It is in these unanswered questions that I see through the centuries of writers, philosophers, theologians, and the like, that not much has changed in the hearts of men. It is presumed that evolution is taking place and it does in varying categories of life, particularly in science and technology where the current knowledge capitulates to the greater and more advanced knowledge.

Man's heart, however, has not evolved. One may tend to believe that we are more civilized than our forefathers. Tell that to the soldiers, or, to the terrorists. Our weapons of war have evolved, but our inhumanity to man has not. Men still argue, fight, try to take that which is not theirs, and make war. We make good war and we strive to make war good. The reflections of the soldier in his call to duty are seen as necessary. It is necessary for us to protect ourselves from the onslaught of evil. The eastern front is not going away. Its desire is to annihilate what is not like itself, so much so that the worship of Molech is continued through the child sacrifice of suicide bombing.

The Dissolution of Truth

Where do the hearts lie in our government leaders? Lord Acton's dictum, 'Power tends to corrupt, absolute power corrupts absolutely,' is in full charge in the hearts of our leaders. Even the minutest foibles in the hearts of our leaders are exacerbated by power. Power is an aromatic incense burning in the nostrils of the political, religious, financial, and educational construct. Power is powerful. How many humans do I need power over to make me worthy of its grasp? Again, more is the answer.

Thomas Jefferson stated, "What country before ever existed a century & half without a rebellion? & what country can preserve its liberties if its rulers are not warned from time to time that their people preserve the spirit of resistance? Let them take arms. The remedy is to set them right as to facts, pardon, and pacify them. What signify a few lives lost in a century or two? The tree of liberty must be refreshed from time to time with the blood of patriots & tyrants. It is its natural manure." [1] Jefferson also stated "I have never been able to conceive how any rational being could propose happiness to himself from the exercise of power over others." [2]

And I, too, "have sworn on the altar of God eternal hostility against every form of tyranny over the mind of man." [3] Thomas Paine wrote, "We must not confuse the peoples with their governments; especially the English people with its government." [4]

Leo Tolstoy, in 1893, wrote a book called, "The Kingdom of God is Within You...Christianity Not as a Mystical Teaching but as a New Concept of Life". This treatise of his was to get at the real truth of Christ's teaching and to depart from the traditional church teaching, the oral and written laws of men, so to speak, that had been created over the centuries by self-serving clerics dressed in Christianity, but were far from it. In the book, Tolstoy, details the injustice performed at the children's expense to train them up in the name of RELIGION, but not necessarily Jesus Christ. He states, "Churchmen substitute for Christianity the version they have framed for themselves, and this view of Christianity they regard as the one infallible one." He also says, "And therefore the churches will not for an instant relax their zeal in the business of hypnotizing grown-up people and deceiving children. This, then, is the work of the churches: to instill a false interpretation of Christ's teaching into men, and to prevent a true interpretation of it for the majority of so-called believers." [5]

Even as Paine stated to the French not to confuse the government with its people, Tolstoy admonishes his reader not to confuse Christianity with so many versions of the church. It is the leaders and their teachings that make the difference. Blatant false teachings on every side creating cult-like matter wrapped in power and prestige are always resting on the hearts of men who deceive at the expense of their followers. The 'next election' is always the best time to demonstrate how faulty these talebearers operate within the confines of their reflexive domain. 'I will say whatever I need to say to get elected,' says the seeker of the office who will yet again prove that he is a 'blundering amateur' as Mr. Krauthammer so eloquently describes.

Liberal leaders of all types that are caught up within their own domains possess an oblique incredulity regarding themselves. The reflexivity attributes disallow honesty and integrity resulting in self-deception. The salesman believes his own lies, which makes him a better salesman. After all, there is too much to lose by telling the truth.

It is the truth that we all need and need to live by; not one man's version of it, but the truth that we need not be ashamed of. It causes

The Dissolution of Truth

me the most destructive distress to know of a child abused. Abuse comes in various forms from the physical and emotional, to the mental and the irrational. Power over a child's mind is opportunistic and deviant, coercive and demeaning. Being in the church for over 55 years, I have seen the best of loving teaching and I have seen the worst of cultic lies. I am a father of three children and I have seen myself at my worst and at my best; my children have eyes and ears. I am a leader in my community and in my home.

Have I, as a leader, told the truth? Have I, as a father, lived the truth? Am I willing to pay the price for being faithful to the Truth as He sees it, foregoing whatever device man may try to conceive in my mind? We are all seed bearers and sowers, none of us are exempt and none of us are without sin. It is the tales we choose to tell that lie at the doorstep of the hearts of our children. A version of the truth is insufficient.

Terry Lursen

A True Leader Must Have Courage

On a day of days in the day of our time, one must not relegate the past to oblivion and say it isn't so. If Tolstoy, Ghandi, and King stood for anything, it was for truth to prevail in the power of peace.

Courage within the ranks sees courage on its face and when courage is dismissed or simply does not reveal itself, the leader is absent not only in heart but in presence. The rank and file show themselves to be just that in a leaderless fight. There are battles to be won and lost, but without the courageous leader to go before in courage, the field of battle is taken by the swift who make themselves aware of what lies ahead. It is to the courageous leader that vision is transplanted into the hearts of the weak and the following in order for peace to come to pass in its time.

Peace does not come without travail and the visionary must recognize his own fate and be willing to pay the price of peace in the denial of self. It takes an "other" worldly type to lead to the other world of what true sustenance looks like. The visionary knows this for sure. But why the wait? Why does this courageous leader take upon himself the virtue of patience while others see their demise?

Has his time come or is he waiting upon another? The relegation of patience must be to the many as well as to the one. Without the courageous leader, dispersion is imminent. Sight must see the inev-

The Dissolution of Truth

itable, it is the due course of internal reconciliation. Better the man stand in due time and even better that the people in waiting stand down for the right time and season to come upon them. Privy is for all in due time.

To the one, I say, take courage and take courage you must when you must and not before. But you also must not wait another moment beyond the time of courage. Go to the mirror of truth and look at what you see. While you are glancing, corruption will knock on your door and you must let it pass knowing that the time has come for a peaceful walk of travail.

Consider it not a time of violence, but of strength. Consider it not a time of war, but of resolve. Consider it not a time of death, but of life for true life lies beyond the mirror, it lies in the hearts of your children.

Always speak the truth and do not lie. Be of good courage and do not fear. Protect those who cannot protect themselves, the unborn, the children and the elderly. Be the man, or woman, that God has purposed you to be and do not grow weary in well doing for God's eyes are upon us all and taking note of all that He sees.

Terry Lursen

A Sphere of Influence

As I continue to read and watch the news and read posts posted on social media, I cannot help but see the lack of influence that the majority of us have on the thoughts, acts, and behaviors of others. Certain leaders and certain media outlets have been given a tremendous amount of influence over the minds of quite a few folk as the very same media outlets continue to portray the results of their influence peddling to the ones that support their views. Lies beget chaos and anger begets violence as the truth of a matter becomes as a vapor lifting higher and higher out of sight and out of reach.

What I see is not so much the impact of detrimental influence, but the resulting vacuum of righteous influence. Is it too late in our nation to be righteously influential before matters occur? I don't think so, for that is the reason why I continue to preach the Gospel.

But am I "influential"?

After all, is not the argument being argued at the moment one of "What is right?" and "What is the truth?"

"Every way of a man is right in his own eyes, but the Lord weighs the hearts." (Proverbs 21:2, NKJV)

Am I Influential as a result of right thinking and leading or as a result of the insatiable personal need for significance and the desire to

The Dissolution of Truth

leave a legacy that I choose to leave rather than what God has chosen in the arrangement of my circumstances?

Righteousness, right thinking and Truth are only found in Jesus Christ and, as such, the majority of our laws were construed on the basis of a moral, ethical and Biblical construct.

It is today as it has been in the past that we find leaderless leaders who do not know right from wrong, truth from error and a lack of conscience towards that which our nation was built upon and remains to be to this day. It is the building up of the SELF that I see in our local, state and national leaders whether it be in the religious or the political realms.

It is past time that those who know what is right and what is true to open their mouths and move their feet towards righteous thinking and righteous expression leading to influencing others to right thinking behaviors. It is past time, indeed.

Be encouraged that Truth that is found in Jesus Christ. The Kingdom of God is being preached and taught and, if you didn't before, you now have the keys to continue Christ's story for He, Himself, went about the countryside preaching and teaching the Kingdom of God. Allow Him to be Himself in you. Abide in Him and He has promised to abide in you. Never cease to pray for yourself, your spouse, your children, your leaders both far and wide. Pray, never cease to pray. It can never get too bad to pray, so, pray in the power of the Holy Spirit for the people of our nation to turn to God, in Jesus Christ.

Terry Lursen

Take the time to investigate what your part is in these matters. One person can make a difference in people's lives. You can be that person.

Take the time to evaluate the gifts and talents that our Lord has placed within you to further His Kingdom, to do good to others, to protect the innocent and to fight for the unborn; to educate in righteousness and to take a stand where a stand is needed. Always vote.

Take the time to invest in yourself, your family, your community and your nation with thoughtful prayer, due diligence to service and making a contribution of your time, talents and other resources that are at your disposal. We all have something to contribute towards doing what is right and good in our homes and communities.

Don't just do something, or anything, but be specific about what you intend to do for our nation. Pray about what you and your family can do. Seek the resources to make it come to fruition and make it happen. The children of our nation need us to help them, educate them, love, nurture and care for them.

And, may the peace of God be upon us all, our families and our nation, in Him. Amen. God bless America.

References of Material - Footnotes

Chapter 1 – The Dissolution of Truth

[1] Voltaire, The Best Known Works of Voltaire (New York: Blue Ribbon Books, 1927) p. 455.

"The Pluralism Project" Harvard University, www.pluralism.org

Chapter 2 – Reflexivity Exposed

[1] Thomas, William I.: Thomas, Dorothy: The Child in America (Alfred Knopf, 1929, 2nd Edition) p. 572.

[2] Ibid.

[3] Voltaire

[4] Paine, Thomas, Thomas Paine Collection, Rights of Man (Forgotten Books, 2007) p. 73

Chapter 5 - The Power of Charismatic Personalities

[1] Tolstoy, Leo, The Kingdom of God Is Within You (Wildside Press, LLC, 2006) p. 79

[2] Chambers, Oswald, The Complete Works of Oswald Chambers (Grand Rapids: Discovery House Publishers, 2000) p. 1468.

Chapter 6 – Kings and Pawns

[1] Webster's New Collegiate Dictionary , (Springfield, 1975).

[2] Chambers, Oswald, p. 1468.

[3] Jefferson, Thomas, Writings of Thomas Jefferson , (New York: Literary Classics of the United States, Inc., 1984) p. 19.

[4] Paine, Thomas, p. 104.

Chapter 9 – The Power of Perspective

[1] Nietzsche, Friedrich, The Will to Power , (New York: Vintage Books, 1968) p. 267.

[2] Ibid., p. 267.

[3] Ibid., p. 267.

[4] Webster's Dictionary, Ibid.

Chapter 11 – Social Liberalism - [1] Paine, p. 15, 16.

[2] Aristotle, The Philosophy of Aristotle , (New York: Signet Classics, 2011) p. 18.

Chapter 12 – Defying Ubiquity

[1] Chambers, p. 719.

Chapter 13 – Speaking the Truth on Marriage

[1] Aristotle, p. 55.

[2] Aristotle, p. 55.

Chapter 14 – Led By Convictions

[1] Tolstoy, p. 134.

Chapter 15 – Who Instituted Marriage

[1] Henry, Matthew, <u>Matthew Henry's Concise Commentary on the Whole Bible</u>, (Grand Rapids: Zondervan Publishing House, 1992) Malachi 2:10-17, p. 1231.

Chapter 16 – The Unbecoming of America

[1] Foucault, Michel, <u>The Order of Things</u>, (New York: Vintage Books, 1994) p. 241.

[2] Aristotle, p. 78.

[3] Aristotle, p. 59.

Chapter 17 – On Personal Relationships

[1] Epictetus, <u>101 Great Philosophers: Makers of Modern Thought</u>, (New York: MJF Books, 2009) p. 41.

Chapter 18 – The Dynamics of Spiritual Truth

[1] Chambers, p. 1016.

[2] Pascal, <u>101 Great Philosophers: Makers of Modern Thought</u>, (New York: MJF Books, 2009) p. 74.

Chapter 22 – Peace- The Treasure That You Seek

[1] Bonhoeffer, Dietrich, <u>The Cost of Discipleship</u>, (New York: The Macmillan Company, 1963) p. 189.

Chapter 26 – Amendment One of the United States Constitution

[1] Jefferson, Thomas, Jefferson's Letter to the Danbury Baptists, p. 510.

Chapter 34 – The Certain Uncertainty of Man

[1] Lewis, C. S., <u>The Abolition of Man</u>, (New York: Simon & Schuster, Touchstone, 1996) p. 20.

Chapter 38 – The Consequence of Corruption - [1] Jefferson, p. 911

[2] Ibid.

[3] Ibid.

[4] Paine, p. 62.

[5] Tolstoy, p. 60-61.

Bibliography

<u>101 Great Philosophers: Makers of Modern Thought</u> , New York: MJF Books, 2009.

Aristotle <u>The Philosophy of Aristotle</u> . New York: Signet Classics, 2011.

Bonhoeffer, Dietrich <u>The Cost of Discipleship</u> New York: The Macmillan Company, 1963.

Chambers, Oswald <u>The Complete Works of Oswald Chambers</u> Grand Rapids: Discovery House Publishers, 2000.

Foucault, Michel <u>The Order of Things</u> New York: Vintage Books, 1994.

Henry, Matthew <u>Matthew Henry Commentary</u> Grand Rapids: Zondervan Publishing House, 1992.

Jefferson, Thomas <u>Writings of Thomas Jefferson</u> New York: Literary Classics of the United States, Inc., 1984.

Lewis, C. S. <u>The Abolition of Man</u> New York: Simon & Schuster, Touchstone, 1996.

Nietzsche, Friedrich <u>The Will to Power</u> New York: Vintage Books, 1968.

Paine, Thomas <u>Thomas Paine Collection</u> Forgotten Books, 2007.

The Pluralism Project, Harvard University, www.pluralism.org

Thomas, William I. & Thomas, Dorothy <u>The Child in America</u> Alfred Knopf, 1929, 2nd Edition.

Tournier, Dr. Paul The Person Reborn New York: Harper & Row, 1966.

Tolstoy, Leo <u>The Kingdom of God Is Within You</u> Wildside Press, LLC., 2006.

Voltaire, <u>The Best Known Works of Voltaire</u> New York: Blue Ribbon, 1927.

<u>Webster's New Collegiate Dictionary</u> Springfield: G & C Merriam Co., 1975.

More Books Written By

Terry Lursen and TEL Publishing

The Treasure Within the Kingdom of God - 366 daily readings about abiding in Christ Jesus and the spreading His gospel, the Kingdom of God.

Paperback ISBN: 978-0-9910989-0-3

ebook ISBN: 978-0-9910989-1-0

The Looking Glass Water: The Water That Woos

A novel about a spiritual lake that contains the water that woos, the water that speaks, the water that knows all that you are...

Paperback ISBN: 978-0-9910989-2-7

ebook ISBN: 978-0-9910989-3-4

The Battle for Crested Hill

Allegory set in the spiritual realm detailing the battles fought for the mind and heart of man.

Hardback ISBN: 978-0-9910989-5-8

Paperback ISBN: 978-0-9910989-6-5

ebook ISBN: 978-0-9910989-7-2

www.perspectivesintruth.com

www.ingramcontent.com/pod-product-compliance
Lightning Source LLC
Chambersburg PA
CBHW070619300426
44113CB00010B/1589